D1500765

The purpose of this study guide is to provide supplemental educational material. It is not intended as a substitute or replacement of THE GLASS CASTLE.

Published by SuperSummary, www.supersummary.com

ISBN – 9798667190936

For more information or to learn about our complete library of study guides, please visit http://www.supersummary.com

Please submit any comments, corrections, or questions to: http://www.supersummary.com/support/

TABLE OF CONTENTS

The Glass Castle is a nonfiction memoir published in 2005
by the American journalist Jeannette Walls. The book
chronicles Walls and her three siblings' nomadic and
impoverished upbringing by their severely maladjusted
parents. An enormous critical and popular success, *The
Glass Castle* remained on the *New York Times* Best Seller
list for 260 weeks in hardcover and 440 weeks in
paperback. In 2017, director Destin Daniel Cretton adapted
the book into a film starring Brie Larson, Naomi Watts, and
Woody Harrelson. This study guide refers to 2006 reprint
edition published by Scribner.

At the start of the narrative, the year is 1963. Three-year-
old Jeannette Walls lives in an Arizona trailer park with her
older sister Lori, her younger brother Brian, and her parents
Rex and Rose Mary—referred to henceforth as Mom and
Dad. Dad is a talented and intelligent electrician who
struggles to maintain a job due to his alcoholism,
intransigence, and paranoia. He often makes grand plans
that never come to fruition, like the construction of a
massive solar-powered home he calls the Glass Castle.
Mom has a teaching degree and comes from a wealthy
family, yet she prefers to paint and write all day, even if it
means living in squalor.

After roughly two years of living a nomadic lifestyle across
the American Southwest, the family settles in a small
rented house in Battle Mountain, Nevada. Jeannette now
has a baby sister, Maureen. Life is comparatively stable for
about six months until Dad loses his job and starts spending
his days and nights drinking. Most days, the refrigerator
and pantry are barren, forcing the kids to steal food from
classmates and neighbors. Mom reluctantly gets a job as a
teacher, and relative stability returns to the Walls

household until a delinquent adolescent named Billy Deel attempts to rape eight-year-old Jeannette. The following day, Billy attacks the children with a BB gun, and Jeannette shoots at Billy's feet, driving him away. Later that night, the police arrive and demand that the family speak to the magistrate in the morning. Due to Dad's distrust of authority, he uproots the family once again, this time to a large house in Phoenix that Mom recently inherited after the death of her wealthy mother.

Dad joins an electrician's union and gains employment easily, but he loses a series of jobs until he is finally ejected from the union. His drinking worsens, culminating in a disastrous Christmas Eve bender during which he lights the Christmas tree on fire. At Jeannette's insistence, Dad quits drinking for a few months but soon spirals back into alcoholism. Broke and desperate for a way to manage Dad's drinking, Mom uproots the family to Welch, West Virginia, a deeply impoverished coal mining community and Dad's hometown. The family stays with Dad's parents, Erma and Ted, until one day Jeannette catches Erma sexually assaulting Brian. The kids wonder if Dad, too, was molested by Erma. Erma kicks the family out of her basement, and the Wallses move into a dilapidated house with no indoor plumbing and holes in the ceiling.

After a visit from a social worker, Jeannette all but forces Mom to get a teaching job to ensure that the family stays together. Before long Dad begins to siphon off the family's budget to feed his addictions. Jeannette's apologetic attitude toward her father finally crumbles when Dad uses Jeannette—who is now around 13 years old—to distract a man whom Dad aims to hustle at pool, and the man attempts to rape Jeannette. Jeannette, Lori, and Brian resolve to escape Welch, and over the following year, they save up money doing odd jobs. On the eve of Lori's move to New York City, Dad steals all their savings. Lori finds a way to move to New York anyway, and about a year later, Jeannette follows her. They convince Brian and Maureen to move to New York as well. Lori works as an illustrator, Brian as a foreman, Maureen enrolls in high school, and Jeannette works for a magazine while studying journalism at Barnard College.

Without warning, Mom and Dad arrive in New York. They stay at Lori's until Lori is forced to evict them. After living on the streets, Mom and Dad move into an abandoned tenement with other indigents. Around this time, Jeannette is aghast to learn that Mom owns property in Texas worth a million dollars but refuses to sell it. Meanwhile, Maureen spirals into mental illness and possibly drug abuse. Maureen stabs Mom during an argument and is sentenced to a psychiatric facility upstate. Jeannette barely talks to her parents for a year, until Dad reveals he is dying. Two weeks later, he suffers a fatal heart attack. In a brief coda, Mom, Lori, and Brian have Thanksgiving dinner at the home Jeannette owns with her husband, John. In a toast, Mom says life with their father was "never boring."

Chapters 1-15

Part 1: "A Woman on the Street"

Chapter 1 Summary

On a cold March day in New York City, as a taxi drives her to a social gathering, Jeannette Walls spots her mother dressed in rags, rummaging through a dumpster. A few days later, Jeanette and Mom meet at a Chinese restaurant. When Jeannette asks what she can do to help, Mom tells her, "I'm fine. You're the one who needs help. Your values are all confused" (6).

Part 2: "The Desert"

Chapter 2 Summary

The narrative flashes back to Jeannette's childhood in 1963. Her earliest memory, at the age of three, is of leaning over the stove cooking hot dogs unsupervised. Jeannette lives in a trailer park in Southern Arizona with Mom, Dad, her older sister, Lori, and her younger brother, Brian. Jeannette's dress catches fire. She suffers serious burns on her ribs, stomach, and chest.

After Jeannette receives skin grafts from her legs, the nurses and doctors tell her she is lucky to be alive. Jeannette loves the hospital because she never runs out of food there. A few days later, Dad absconds with Jeannette in the middle of the night, whiskey on his breath.

Chapter 3 Summary

Within days, Jeannette is back to cooking hot dogs for herself unsupervised. Mom commends her for getting "right back in the saddle" (15).

Chapter 4 Summary

A few months later, Dad rouses the whole family in the middle of the night to say they have 15 minutes to gather their belongings and abandon the trailer park. "Doing the skedaddle" (19), as Jeannette calls it, is a frequent occurrence for the transient Walls family, which never stays in one place for more than a few months.

Chapter 5 Summary

Dad's insistence on relocating every few months is in large part a product of his paranoia over a series of adversaries, real and imagined. These include but are not limited to the Mafia, the FBI, Standard Oil, and the police, which he refers to as "the gestapo." Although Dad has no college degree, he is a talented electrician and engineer who finds employment with various mining companies around the Southwest. Wherever he goes, he tends to make enemies one way or another, through unpaid gambling debts or by getting into drunken brawls.

Dad promises the family that their lifestyle of transient poverty will end as soon as he acquires the investment money to build his grand and ingenious invention: the Prospector. The Prospector will automatically sift gold nuggets out of the dirt using a complicated system of weights. Dad also has ambitious plans to build the Glass Castle, a solar-powered home in the desert made entirely of glass. Although everyone in the family agrees Dad is brilliant, they also recognize he has what Mom calls "a little bit of a drinking situation" (23).

Chapter 6 Summary

Here, Jeannette broadly traces the history of her immediate family. Dad hails from a small West Virginia coal-mining town called Welch. When Jeannette's parents met, Dad was in the Air Force, and Mom was a beautiful USO model who came from a wealthy family in Texas. After numerous rejections, Mom finally wears down and agrees to marry Dad.

A few months later, Mom is pregnant with Lori. Three years later, Jeannette is born, and a year after that, Brian arrives. With so many children to support and so little money, Dad pawns Mom's wedding ring without asking her, a ring Mom's wealthy mother, Grandma Smith, purchased.

Chapter 7 Summary

About a year after the hot dog incident, when Jeannette is four and Lori is seven, the family drives to Las Vegas in the Green Caboose, a car Dad purchased to replace the Blue Goose after it died. With an intoxicated Dad behind the wheel, the Green Caboose violently rolls over a set of railroad tracks, causing the backseat door to open and Jeannette to fall out of the car. With her body covered in cuts embedded with gravel, Jeannette watches as the Green Caboose rolls around a bend, leaving her behind. After waiting for what feels like hours in the hot sun, the Green Caboose finally returns. Though initially enraged, Jeannette cannot help but laugh uproariously when Dad says, "Damn, honey. You busted your snot locker pretty good" (31).

Chapter 8 Summary

For about a month, the family lives in a dingy Las Vegas
motel room while Dad works the blackjack tables at the
casino. One day, Dad tells the family a blackjack dealer has
figured out his system, and now they all must flee the city
to escape the Mafia. They drive to San Francisco, where
Dad hopes to find investors for the Prospector. The family
settles in a flophouse in the Tenderloin district.

One night, after spending much of the day playing with
matches in the bathroom, Jeannette wakes up to see the
curtains of their room on fire. The family escapes, but the
flophouse burns down. Dad vows to abandon the city
without having obtained his startup cash and to resettle the
family in the desert.

Chapter 9 Summary

Near the Eagle Mountains in California, Mom insists that
they stop at an ancient Joshua tree so she can paint it.
Jeannette finds its "permanent state of windblownness"
ugly (35). Later, when Jeannette finds a Joshua tree sapling,
she vows to protect it from the wind so it grows tall and
straight, but Mom forbids her from doing so, telling her,
"It's the Joshua tree's struggle that gives it its beauty" (38).

The family rents a tiny house in nearby Midland, a small
mining community. Mom becomes pregnant again. She
also redoubles her artistic efforts, spending all day painting,
writing, and making sculptures out of the gypsum Dad
brings home from his new mining job.

Chapter 10 Summary

After an argument with his foreman, Dad loses his job at the gypsum factory. With no money to buy Christmas presents, Dad asks the children to point to any star in the sky to receive as a gift. Jeannette picks Venus, and after some convincing, Dad agrees she can have a planet for Christmas. When the Sun cools and everyone is forced to leave Earth for Venus, he says, they will need Jeannette's permission.

Chapter 11 Summary

In anticipation of Mom giving birth, the family relocates to Blythe, a significantly larger town 20 miles South with two movie theaters and two state prisons. Two months into their stay in Blythe, Mom gives birth to a baby girl, Maureen. Upon holding Maureen for the first time, Jeannette says, "I promised her I'd always take care of her" (46).

Chapter 12 Summary

A few months later, a police officer tries to pull over Dad over a broken taillight. Because he has no registration or insurance, Dad speeds off, eventually evading the cop. After this close call, he decides it's time for the family to move on once again, this time to Battle Mountain, Nevada.

Chapter 13 Summary

On the outskirts of Battle Mountain, the family moves into an old wooden train depot that's been converted into a domicile. It has a bathtub but no toilets. For furniture, the family uses old spools and crates they recover from junkyards. The children sleep in cardboard boxes. When a discussion is raised over whether to buy the children real beds, Mom decides instead that they should buy a piano. Dad purchases one from a closed down saloon, but they cannot get it inside the house. The piano will sit outside in the yard for the duration of the family's stay in Battle Mountain.

Chapter 14 Summary

Dad finds work as an electrician at a barite mine. Although he visits the local bar, the Owl Club, with some regularity, Dad spends most nights at home with the kids. Each evening, the whole family sprawls out on the floor reading books, with a dictionary in the center of the room used to look up unfamiliar words.

Chapter 15 Summary

Mom and Dad enroll the three eldest children in school. They give their children very few rules except that they must be home by dark. On rare occasions when a rule is broken, Dad will beat Jeannette or the others with a belt, but never out of anger, Jeannette insists. She also spends hours wandering the desert collecting rocks, her favorite of which are rare geodes.

One day, Jeannette and Brian bring a series of toxic chemicals they recovered from the dump to an abandoned shed they name the laboratory. Jeannette lights the chemicals on fire, causing a plume of flames to set the shed ablaze. Jeannette escapes, but Brian is trapped. Dad manages to save Brian from the burning building just in time. As they watch the shed burn, Dad points out how the invisible heat at the tops of the flames distorts the image of the desert beyond, referring to it as "the boundary between turbulence and order" (61).

Chapters 1-15 Analysis

The central question at the heart of these chapters—and one that extends throughout the remainder of the book—is this: What causes two individuals, both of whom are presumably in possession of the intellectual means to thrive in society, to live on its margins and to subject their children to such a life? There are no easy answers to this question. If *The Glass Castle* was a work of fiction, a reader could more readily look for clues in the author's storytelling and characterization choices. Perhaps the answer would be equally elusive, but at least then the reader could attribute this to intent on the part of the author. Because *The Glass Castle* is a nonfiction memoir, the reader must take the facts at face value to a certain extent. These things happened, and it is not necessarily Walls's job—neither as a writer nor as a human being—to explain the reasons behind her parents' actions. In fact, if the book is any indication, Walls is as conflicted and perplexed as the reader when it comes to diagnosing her parents' motivations.

That said, there are a number of possibilities worth considering to explain Mom and Dad's seemingly incomprehensible behavior. Perhaps the most obvious explanation is substance abuse, the consequences of which constitute one of the book's major themes. Even at this early stage of the novel, when the narrator is too young to understand alcoholism at a clinical level, Jeannette knows that Dad has a drinking problem, one that Mom euphemistically calls "a drinking situation" (23). Most of the time—that is, when Dad drinks beer—life is "a little bit scary but still a lot of fun" (23). When Dad drinks liquor, Jeannette watches him become "an angry-eyed stranger who threw around furniture and threatened to beat up Mom or anyone else who got in his way" (23).

An addict like Dad whose life so persistently revolves around procuring and consuming his drug of choice will likely struggle to maintain steady employment and housing, but to attribute the chaos of the Walls clan to substance abuse alone is insufficient, particularly given the fact that Mom "didn't drink anything stronger than tea" (29). Indeed, Mom's motivations are much more difficult to reckon with, especially later on, when the full magnitude of the financial assets at her disposal comes to light. Mom's own pithy explanation for her willingness to live in a state of transient squalor is that she's "an excitement addict" (93). One can therefore see the contours of her codependent relationship with Dad take shape, as her antipathy toward boredom enables Dad's irresponsible rabblerousing. However, "excitement addict" isn't exactly a rigorous diagnosis, and it is therefore worth exploring the deeper psychological factors behind Mom's behavior.

For example, both Mom and Dad are severe nonconformists with innate distrust of authority. Though Mom is less paranoid than Dad, this distrust likely makes it easier for Mom to entertain and tolerate his ramblings about the Mafia, the FBI, and the police offers supposedly out to get him. Her anti-authority bent extends to her approach toward childrearing. Walls writes, "Mom believed that children shouldn't be burdened with a lot of rules and restrictions" (59). This statement could also be seen as a justification for Mom's failure to nurture her children. That attitude is mostly strongly reflected symbolically when Jeannette finds a small Joshua tree sapling. She writes, "I wanted to dig it up and replant it near our house. I told Mom that I would protect it from the wind and water it every day so that it could grow nice and tall and straight" (38). To Mom, however, this idea is a betrayal of her values. She tells Jeannette, "You'd be destroying what makes it special. [...] It's the Joshua tree's struggle that gives it its beauty" (38). Mom fetishizes struggle, perhaps as a coping mechanism for her own difficult circumstances.

Another symbol introduced in these chapters is the Glass Castle—a symbol so important that Walls names her book after it. In describing it, Walls writes:

> It would have a glass ceiling and thick glass walls and even a glass staircase. The Glass Castle would have solar cells on the top that would catch the sun's rays and convert them into electricity for heating and cooling and running all the appliances. It would even have its own water-purification system (25).

At its most basic level, the Glass Castle represents the epitome of the lifestyle Dad would like to lead, one that is fully sustainable, self-sufficient, and beholden to no authority aside from nature itself. As the book goes on, it also comes to represent the increasingly illusory hope that Dad will fulfill his many broken promises. For example, Walls writes, "That was why we had to find gold. To get Mom a new wedding ring. That and so we could build the Glass Castle" (28). This subtle juxtaposition reveals the extent to which a perfectly achievable goal—like keeping a job long enough to save up for a new wedding ring—is, in Dad's hands at least, as preposterous as building the Glass Castle. At the same time, the Glass Castle is such an exciting and magical prospect that it is serves as fodder for Jeannette's persistent illusion of Dad as the greatest father on Earth.

On this note, it is important to consider Walls's narration technique. At this stage of the book, Jeannette is still a child, and the narration reflects her youth. To her, there is nothing odd about a three-year-old cooking hot dogs unsupervised, or a family that moves over a dozen times in half that many years, or children using cardboard boxes as beds. As Jeannette grows older and begins to understand more clearly how other children live, she offers more of her own judgments of her parents' behavior. At this point, the narration still depends on the wide chasm between Jeannette's matter-of-fact observations and an adult reader's understanding of neglect to illustrate the severity of the family's circumstances.

This perception of neglect also plays into another theme: the extent to which neglect is abuse. To be sure, there is little malice on the part of either parent, at least at this point in the book. Both Mom and Dad seem convinced that their approach toward parenting is the best way to facilitate their children's happiness and well-being. Particularly as the narrative progresses, however, it will become clear that their lifestyle is the result of selfishness, manifested by Dad's alcoholism and Mom's unwillingness to sacrifice her "career" as an artist.

These chapters also introduce Christmas as a recurring motif. At different intervals of the book, Christmas is a time when the Walls family dynamics are laid bare. During these early chapters, Jeannette still thinks of the Wallses' impoverished and transient existence as an adventure and even a badge of honor. This sense is strongly reflected in the joy she feels when Dad, unable to afford presents because he lost his job, gives Jeannette the planet Venus for Christmas. She writes:

> We laughed about all the kids who believed in the
> Santa myth and got nothing for Christmas but a
> bunch of cheap plastic toys. 'Years from now, when
> all the junk they got is broken and long forgotten,'
> Dad said, 'you'll still have your stars' (41).

A final recurring motif introduced here is that of turbulence and order. Dad describes the tops of the flames that leap out of the shack Jeannette and Brian set aflame as the boundary between turbulence and order. He adds, "It's a place where no rules apply, or at least they haven't figured 'em out yet. You-all got a little too close to it today" (61). This is a fitting metaphor for the lives of the Walls family, and in particular Dad's life. Dad is most comfortable with chaos, and so whenever the family improves its fortunes enough to come into proximity with stability—that is, to exist within that boundary between turbulence and order—Dad finds a way to sabotage himself and the rest of the Walls clan. It is clearly not a state Dad is comfortable with, both because of his inherently chaotic personality and perhaps also because he is deeply insecure about his ability to provide for his family. This insecurity may also be why all of Dad's plans for lifting his family out of chaos involve gambits that range between unlikely and impossible, like finding gold and building the Glass Castle. It is easier for him to be driven by impossible hopes than it is to do the hard work of navigating one's way out of turbulence and into order.

Chapters 16-22

Chapter 16 Summary

On the way home from school, Jeannette and Brian frequently pass an establishment known as the Green Lantern. Eager to know what goes on there, Jeannette sends Brian to talk to a woman smoking a cigarette on the porch wearing revealing clothing. The woman tells Brian it's a place where "men came in and women there were nice to them" (63).

Chapter 17 Summary

One day, the family visits the Hot Pot, a natural sulfur spring that smells like rotten eggs. Brian and Lori swim readily, but Jeannette is too scared to do so. Over and over, Dad tosses Jeannette into the middle of the spring, causing burning water to enter her throat and eyes. Eventually, upon being thrown in the spring for the umpteenth time, Jeannette becomes so angry at Dad that she successfully evades his attempts to recover her, thus learning to swim.

Chapter 18 Summary

Dad keeps his job at the barite mine for six months—a record for him. More and more, Dad disappears for days at a time. Aside from the proceeds of an occasional odd job or gambling win, the family has no income. As such, the family's refrigerator is frequently barren. To stave off hunger, Jeannette steals items from her classmates' lunches during recess. One day, Jeannette comes home to see Lori eating margarine and sugar with a spoon, saying it tastes like frosting. Jeannette suspects Mom of hiding food from the kids so she can eat it herself later. When Jeannette complains of her hunger—breaking Mom's one rule that life be treated as an adventure—Mom considers hitting her and then breaks down in tears instead.

That evening, a massive fight erupts between Mom and Dad that lasts all through the night and into the next morning. Mom accuses Dad of spending all day drinking at the Owl Club instead of looking for work. Dad demands that Mom use her teaching degree to a get a job at the local school, but Mom refuses, reemphasizing that she is an artist. As practically the whole town listens to the clamor from out front, one of Mom's paintings flies through an upstairs window, followed by her easel. Next, Mom hangs from the windowsill, fighting Dad as he tries to pull her back inside.

Chapter 19 Summary

The next morning, Mom applies for and obtains employment as a teacher at Battle Mountain's intermediate school. Mom hates teaching, in part because she doesn't like making lesson plans nor answering to authority. Most of all she hates it because her mother forced her to get a teaching degree as something to fall back on should she fail as an artist.

Chapter 20 Summary

At first, Mom's teaching salary allows the fridge to be regularly stocked. Increasingly, however, Dad demands the majority of Mom's paychecks, and she embarks on increasingly elaborate schemes to hide her money from him. While Brian and Lori adopt an increasingly cynical attitude toward Dad, Jeannette continues to defend him.

One day, as Jeannette and Brian pass the Green Lantern, a woman named Ginger waves to Brian, who receives her coldly. When Jeannette asks him why, Brian explains that, on his birthday, Dad made Brian wait in a motel anteroom while he and Ginger remained in the bedroom for a long time. When they left the bedroom, Dad forced Brian to give Ginger the comic book he received for his birthday because she was a fan of the series and it was "the gentlemanly thing to do" (79).

Chapter 21 Summary

Not long after Jeannette's eighth birthday, an 11-year-old boy named Billy Deel moves into the neighborhood with his father. Rumored to be a juvenile delinquent and possibly a sociopath, Billy follows Jeannette everywhere and tells their classmates the two of them are dating. Although Jeannette hates the way Billy disrespects his father, Mom tells Jeannette to be friends with him anyway.

During a game of Hide and Seek, Billy enters a shed where Jeannette is hiding. He forces himself on top of her and attempts to rape her. Jeannette bites Billy hard on the ear, and he punches her in the face, causing her nose to bleed. She escapes the shed and runs home. The next day, while Mom and Dad are away at the Owl Club, Billy arrives at Jeannette's house with a BB gun. He breaks the window to gain entry and shoots Jeannette in the ribs. As the four children hide behind an overturned spool table, Lori runs upstairs and retrieves Dad's pistol. She shoots at Billy, but he evades the bullet by leaping out the window. From 50 yards away, Billy resumes shooting at them with the BB gun. Jeannette takes the pistol from Lori and shoots at Billy's feet, and he runs away.

Later on, Mom and Dad arrive in a squad car. Although the children explain that they shot at Billy out of self-defense, a police officer insists that the family come to the courthouse the following morning. With that, Mom and Dad announce that they are leaving Battle Mountain that night and moving to Phoenix, where Grandma Smith lives.

Chapter 22 Summary

As the family leaves Battle Mountain, Jeannette looks forward to seeing Grandma Smith again. When she asks if they plan to stay at her house, however, she receives the startling news that Grandma Smith died. Instead, the family will live in an adobe house in the city's business district that Mom inherited. Also part of her inheritance is a significant sum of money. Certain that her art career will thrive in Phoenix, Mom calls Billy Deel "a blessing in disguise" (93).

Chapters 16-22 Analysis

In these chapters, the reader begins to sense the adventure of the Wallses' lifestyle transform into a nightmare. The process is slow at first. Having finally settled for a prolonged period in one place, Jeannette is able to better observe how other families differ from hers. For example, her friend Carla's mother hangs adhesive strips to get rid of the flies. Mom, however, is content to let the family's increasingly large brood of stray cats eat the flies because it's "the same as buying cat food, only cheaper" (64).

When Dad loses his job at the barite mine, the Wallses' lives no longer feel like they consist of the fun exploits of a merely idiosyncratic family. Sleeping under the stars or living in a house full of wild animals can be romanticized, especially for a child, but starvation cannot. The fight over who will eat the last of the margarine is a particularly galling illustration of the devastating effects of hunger. That scene culminates in a telling exchange between Jeannette and Mom. At one point, Jeannette expresses the fact that she is hungry, yet despite the fact that this sentiment has been expressed millions of times by far more privileged children than her, Mom responds to it with outrage. The author writes, "I'd broken one of our unspoken rules: We were always supposed to pretend our life was one long and incredibly fun adventure" (69). Mom's outrage, however, quickly dissipates into tears. True, Mom may be an "excitement addict," as she says, but this exchange reflects the extent to which her tendency to view life as an adventure is a coping mechanism for maintaining a relationship with a man as toxic and irresponsible as Dad.

Still, Jeannette's wide-eyed admiration of Dad persists undeterred. This admiration is put to the test when the family visits the Hot Pot sulfur spring. Dad is not the first parent to teach a child how to swim by tossing them into the deep end, but Dad's persistence, combined with the fact that the water is full of a sulfuric irritant, makes this sequence of events arguably abusive. Dad's reasoning is similar to that used by both himself and Mom at various intervals: that children must overcome their fears. Like many of Mom and Dad's aphorisms, this is true and worthwhile on the surface, but in practice, it works to justify a raft of questionable parenting tactics for both parties. Jeannette is not yet so jaded as to question whether the Hot Pot incident is anything but a reflection of her father's love. She recalls:

> Dad kept telling me that he loved me, that he never would have let me drown, but you can't cling to the side your whole life, that one lesson every parent needs to teach a child is 'If you don't want to sink, you better figure out how to swim.' What other reason, he asked, would possibly make him do this? Once I got my breath back, I figured he must be right. There was no other way to explain it (66).

Jeannette's skewed perspective on her father is also highlighted by the disgust she feels when Billy mocks his own alcoholic father. She even considers it a worthy comeback when she shouts, "My daddy is nothing like your daddy! When my daddy passes out, he *never* pisses himself!" (83).

Less tolerant of Dad's behavior is Brian, whose attitude begins to diverge from Jeannette's in these chapters. The tipping point for Brian arguably involves a far greater betrayal than the Hot Pot incident. It also coincides with a broader loss of innocence, as Jeannette intuits that since his birthday Brian understands more about what goes on at the Green Lantern than she does. As before, Dad justifies his cruelty under the guise of a life lesson, forcing Brian to give the comic book he receives for his birthday to Ginger because "it was the gentlemanly thing to do" (79). The difference between Jeannette's opinion of Dad and Brian's increasingly skeptical attitude toward him is illustrated when Jeannette defends the fact that Dad siphons off so much of Mom's paycheck. She says, "It's not all for booze. Most of it's for research on cyanide leaching," and Brian responds, "Dad doesn't need to do research on leaching. He's an expert" (78).

This series of events surrounding Ginger is also the first in a string of toxic incidents that shape Jeannette's experiences with human sexuality. The second, when Billy attempts to rape Jeannette, is far more disturbing, both literally and symbolically. For example, after Billy tells Jeannette he raped her, she looks up the word "rape" in the dictionary. There is an upsetting symmetry between this scene and an earlier one in which Jeannette uses the dictionary to look up words she doesn't understand from Laura Ingalls Wilder books. This callback emphasizes how quickly Jeannette's innocence erodes under the circumstances of the chaotic life Mom and Dad build for her. It is not their fault Billy sexually assaulted Jeannette, but their selfish attitude toward the incident is laid bare by Mom's characterization of Billy as a "blessing in disguise" (93), given her expectation that her art career will flourish in Phoenix.

The reader also gets a better glimpse in these chapters of Mom's motivations. It is revealed that Grandma Smith compelled Mom to get a teaching degree in case her art career failed. As young artists are sometimes wont to do, Mom views this as a major affront reflecting a lack of faith in her artistic abilities. Thus, her reluctant decision to get a teaching job—and her poor performance of the duties of said job—are rooted in deep resentment toward Grandma Smith. Mom's history with Grandma Smith is an important piece of context when considering her motivations. From her slavish devotion to art, to her lack of rule enforcement when raising her children, Mom seeks to exhibit all of the opposite qualities of Grandma Smith—an understandable impulse, perhaps, but one that becomes increasingly hard to defend as the family falls deeper into poverty.

Chapters 23-28

Chapter 23 Summary

Jeannette and her family's new home is massive by any standard, containing 14 rooms. Mom converts the two front rooms into the R.M. Walls Art Studio. The kids attend a public school called Emerson where they are all in gifted classes. Dad joins the local electricians' union and lands a job easily amid Phoenix's booming economy.

Their new life isn't one of total luxury, however. The house is infested with cockroaches and termites, and before long the living room floor looks like Swiss cheese. Dad does little to address the termite problem aside from hammering his empty beer cans into the holes in the floor.

Chapter 24 Summary

At night, Mom and Dad refuse to close the windows, insisting that the kids need fresh air. One night, a man climbs through the window and rubs his hands on Jeannette's genitals while she sleeps. Brian chases the man off with a hatchet, but still Dad and Mom insist on keeping the windows open.

Despite her anti-authority bent, Mom thinks of herself as a devout Catholic. Most Sundays, she takes the kids to mass. The family finds little sense of community there, however, thanks to Dad's frequent heckling of the priest.

Chapter 25 Summary

Life in the city is hard on Dad, who misses the wide-open spaces of the family's previous homes. One day, he takes the whole family to the zoo. Outside the cheetah enclosure, Dad climbs over a fence and rests his hand on the animal's neck through the bars. Jeannette follows him and asks to pet the cheetah, which proceeds to lick her hand. As a security guard escorts the family out of the zoo, Jeannette recalls, "I could hear people around us whispering about the crazy drunk man and his dirty little urchin children, but who cared what they thought? None of them had ever had their hand licked by a cheetah" (109).

Chapter 26 Summary

Not long after the cheetah incident, Dad loses his job. With Mom's inheritance money gone, the family returns to a life of indigence. Jeannette and Brian survive on one meal a day at school, plus whatever they find in dumpsters. Meanwhile, Dad embarks on a righteous crusade to rid Phoenix of the mob, spending his days and nights doing "research" at bars supposedly run by the Mafia. Increasingly, he comes home in fits of drunken rage, breaking furniture and dishes.

The family approaches Christmas that year with great anticipation. They even buy a Christmas tree for one dollar after the man at the tree farm takes pity on them. On Christmas Eve, although Dad is so drunk he can barely stand, Mom insists he accompany the family to midnight mass. Dad interrupts the mass with a series of blasphemous outbursts, and the family is asked to leave.

Back home, Jeannette gives Dad an antique lighter as a present. He uses it to light the tree on fire. As Dad laughs uproariously, the rest of the family frantically extinguishes the fire with water and blankets, ruining the rest of the presents.

Chapter 27 Summary

When Dad asks Jeannette what she wants for her 10th birthday, Jeannette says she wants him to quit drinking. The next morning, Dad straps himself to his bed. For almost a week, Dad is in agony, groaning and sweating constantly and occasionally letting out hideous screams. Even after his delirium stops, Dad shakes uncontrollably for days. It takes him most of the summer to recuperate, but by the fall he recovers much of his strength.

To celebrate, Dad plans a family camping trip to the Grand Canyon, just like old times. On the way there, around 80 miles into their trip, Dad tries to see how fast the car will go. White steam shoots out of the hood, and the car clatters to a stop. Unable to fix the engine, the family abandons the car and hitchhikes back to Phoenix. When they reach home, Dad disappears.

Chapter 28 Summary

Dad returns three days later in a drunken fury. When he finds Mom hiding in the tub, she runs downstairs and grabs a butcher knife. After a physical confrontation, the two abruptly stop fighting and fall into each other's embrace.

With Dad drinking again and with no income, Mom decides the family should move to West Virginia where Dad's parents live. With some money Mom receives from an oil lease she inherited, she buys a 1956 Oldsmobile that barely makes it home from the car lot, lurching and stalling the entire time. Mom refuses to either sell or rent out the Phoenix house while they are away. While Dad initially vows to stay in Phoenix, he finally gets in the car moments before the family drives away.

Chapters 23-28 Analysis

The big house and cash inheritance Mom receives after her mother's death would seem to position the Wallses for success—and for a while they do. Eventually, however, the family's stay in Phoenix follows the same pattern as the stay in Battle Mountain. At first, life is an adventure, albeit one with troubling warning signs. Dad's tendency to plug up termite holes with spent beer cans is a particularly literal representation of his attitude toward life's problems. The scene at the zoo when Dad pets the cheetah and invites Jeannette to do the same is another moment of high adventure that nevertheless exists in that space between turbulence and order that is most dangerous for the Wallses. In fact, Dad's act of crossing the fence and putting his hand through the cheetah cage in many ways mirrors his earlier speech about crossing the boundary between safety and chaos.

Dad also willfully crosses that boundary when he once again loses a series of jobs. This most recent slide back into indigence is made all the more tragic because of the potential of the family's fresh start in Phoenix. Jeannette attributes Dad's self-destruction in Phoenix to his inability to thrive in a city. Given that these exploits follow the precisely same pattern as the ones in Battle Mountain and everywhere else, however, this explanation is far from convincing.

As Dad's alcoholism worsens even further, the nature of his codependent relationship with Mom is put into even sharper relief. For example, the author writes:

> After Dad had collapsed, I would try to pick up the place, but Mom always made me stop. She'd been reading books on how to cope with an alcoholic, and they said that drunks didn't remember their rampages, so if you cleaned up after them, they'd think nothing had happened. 'Your father needs to see the mess he's making of our lives,' Mom said. But when Dad got up, he'd act as if all the wreckage didn't exist, and no one discussed it with him (112).

Despite Mom's effort, she has already exhibited a tolerance for living amid squalor and chaos. Therefore, Dad has little reason to bat an eye at the wreckage of his latest bender. While Mom is a victim in a toxic, verbally abusive relationship, her own tendencies toward chaos only serve to feed into and exacerbate Dad's tendencies toward the same.

The family hits another nadir at Christmas—a holiday that, as in earlier chapters, reflects the Wallses' family dynamics at a given moment. Perhaps out of desperation, the family anticipates having the best Christmas of their lives. It turns out to be the worst: Dad drunkenly heckles the priest at

Midnight Mass, sets the Christmas tree on fire, and laughs uproariously while the family douses the flames, thereby ruining the presents. By this point, the family's expectations of Dad are so low that nobody externalizes their anger in the wake of these acts. Jeannette writes, "When Dad went crazy, we all had our own ways of shutting down and closing off, and that was what we did that night" (115).

It may be tempting to view all of the Wallses' problems through the lens of substance abuse, but this interpretation is complicated by the family's aborted trip to the Grand Canyon. Having been sober for months, Dad seeks to take the family on a trip that recalls the more innocent adventuring of years past, but he once again sabotages his and his family's happiness by seeing how fast the car will go, causing it to die 80 miles outside Phoenix. The gambit is not malicious, merely reckless, but it highlights the extent to which alcohol merely exacerbates Dad's inherent need for chaos. The scene also reveals the manner in which Jeannette is perceived by rest of the family as being as much an enabler of Dad as Mom is, as she encourages him to drive "faster than the speed of light" (119). Lori criticizes her over this, but Jeannette is only ten years old at this point. More than anything, Jeannette remains a victim of that same innocence and optimism driving her belief that Dad will one day build the Glass Castle. It is the slow erosion of this innocence that makes up the dominant psychological narrative of the book.

Chapters 29-41

Part 3: "Welch"

Chapter 29 Summary

Before the family even crosses the New Mexico border, the Oldsmobile breaks down. Dad fixes it, but from that point on the car can't drive faster than 20 miles per hour. It takes the family a month to reach Welch, West Virginia, a coal-mining town nestled deep in the heart of Appalachia. When Jeannette meets Dad's obese mother, Erma, his thin father, Ted, and his toothless Uncle Stanley, she initially believes it is a prank—that Dad arranged for "the weirdest people in town to pretend they were his family" (131). Mom, Dad, and the four kids move into Erma's basement.

Chapter 30 Summary

As she recalls her initial tour of Welch, the author points out that the town was so poor, President John F. Kennedy once toured it to illustrate to the rest of the country that starvation-level poverty still exists in America. When the kids ask if they can swim in the Tug River, Dad says that it has "the highest level of fecal bacteria of any river in North America" (133). Ludicrously, Mom concludes that with no competition her art career is poised to take off in Welch.

Chapter 31 Summary

At Welch Elementary, the principal struggles to understand Jeannette and Brian because they speak too fast for him. In turn, they struggle to understand the principal's slow, West Virginian drawl. As such, he enrolls them in remedial classes. Every day at recess and after school, Jeannette suffers verbal and physical bullying at the hands of a group of black girls led by Dinitia Hewitt.

Chapter 32 Summary

The bullying continues, exacerbated by the fact that Jeannette is constantly dirty. Erma only allows the kids to take one bath a week in just four inches of water. One day, Jeannette saves a five-year-old black boy from an angry dog. As she carries the boy to his home on her shoulders, a puzzled Dinitia watches from across the street.

From then on, Dinitia and her friends no longer torment Jeannette. Dinitia even asks Jeannette for help on an English project. When Erma and Ted learn about this, they both use a hateful racial slur. Jeannette says, "You're not supposed to use that word" (143), causing Erma to banish her to the basement without dinner. Despite Mom's progressive attitudes on racial equality, she refuses to come to Jeannette's defense out of fear of getting kicked out of Erma's house.

Chapter 33 Summary

That winter, Mom and Dad drive the Oldsmobile back to Phoenix in hopes of retrieving some of the items they left behind. After a morning of heavy drinking, Erma tells Brian she needs to mend his britches in her bedroom. Upon hearing a struggle, Jeannette enters the bedroom to discover Erma sexually abusing Brian with her hands. After telling Lori what happened, Erma tries to slap Jeannette, but Lori stops her hand. In response, Erma slaps Lori, who proceeds to slap her back. After Stanley breaks them up, Erma banishes the kids to the freezing basement indefinitely with no food except for what Stanley occasionally sneaks down to them.

Weeks later when their parents return, Dad is furious at the kids for back-talking and making up lies about Erma. Jeannette later wonders aloud to Lori and Brian if Erma did the same thing to Dad as a child. Nobody says a word in response.

Chapter 34 Summary

Mom and Dad reveal that they returned to Phoenix to find the house looted. Anything they managed to retrieve had to be abandoned in Nashville when the Oldsmobile died for good, and Mom and Dad were forced to take a bus back to West Virginia. Moreover, the incident with Brian causes Erma to banish the entire family from her home.

Dad finds a tiny rundown house on a steep hillside that the family will pay $1,000 to own, in monthly $50 installments. Although there is a spigot outside, the house has no indoor plumbing or running water. While the house is wired for electricity, the family cannot afford to pay for it. It has a coal stove for cooking and heating but no chimney. Dad insists he bought it for the land, on which he plans to finally build the Glass Castle. Not long after they move in, the ceiling in the kitchen collapses. As Jeannette listens to falling rain from her cardboard mattress, she dreams of Arizona.

Chapter 35 Summary

Jeannette and Brian pass the time by digging a foundation for the Glass Castle. With no money to pay for trash collection, Dad tells Jeannette to throw the family's increasingly large pile of garbage into the foundation hole. In an effort to liven up the house, Jeannette begins to paint the exterior yellow. She manages to paint around three-fourths of the house but is too short to reach the top, even with a rickety ladder. The rest of the family refuses to help, and a cold snap ruins the rest of the paint, leaving the house only partially painted and looking worse than it did before.

Chapter 36 Summary

The family's Hobart Street neighborhood is full of kids, and for the first time Maureen makes plenty of friends. Jeannette is initially receptive to the friendly overtures of a girl named Cindy until she realizes Cindy's intent is to recruit her for a junior chapter of the Ku Klux Klan.

Chapter 37 Summary

Jeannette recalls persistent cascades of violence in Welch: Men beat their wives, wives beat their children, and children beat each other. As the poorest kids in the neighborhood whose father is the town drunk, the Walls children are frequent targets of this violence, especially at the hands of Ernie Goad and his friends. One day, Jeannette and Brian build a mattress catapult that flings rocks down a hill at Ernie and his co-tormentors.

Chapter 38 Summary

The following summer, Dad returns home drunk one night, covered in blood and with gashes on his head and forearm. He guides Jeannette's hand as she sews up the cut on his arm by kerosene light.

Chapter 39 Summary

Dad continues to disappear for days at a time, coming home on occasion with a bag of groceries purchased with gambling winnings or the proceeds from odd jobs. He claims to be working on a more efficient way to burn coal.

The family's only other income comes from Mom's oil lease checks. Jeannette and Brian spend summer days foraging for food, sometimes eating cow feed pilfered from a nearby farm. When school starts in the fall, Jeannette rummages for scraps in the cafeteria garbage can and retreats to a bathroom stall to eat them. Maureen eats dinner virtually every night at one of her many friends' homes.

One night, Brian catches Mom surreptitiously eating a chocolate bar under a blanket. With tears in her eyes, she says, "I can't help it. I'm a sugar addict, just like your father is an alcoholic" (174).

Chapter 40 Summary

That winter, Mom and Dad refuse to spend $50 for enough coal to last the season. Instead, Jeannette and Brian walk up and down the road picking up bits of coal that fall off trucks. With no insulation in the home, any heat they generate from the stove dissipates quickly.

Chapter 41 Summary

Near the end of that winter, Erma dies of liver failure. After the funeral, when Dad doesn't return home for four days, Mom orders Jeannette to track him down. Jeannette enters a series of increasingly squalid bars until she finally sees Dad regaling the locals with tall tales from his Air Force days. Before returning home, Dad insists on taking so many whiskey shots that he can no longer walk. A man offers to drive Jeannette home with Dad passed out in the cab of his pickup truck. On the way, Jeannette tells the man that when she grows up, she wants to be a geology specialist who studies the formation of geodes. He replies, "For the daughter of the town drunk, you sure got big plans" (182).

Two months later, Stanley accidentally burns down his and Ted's house after falling asleep while smoking. Because their new apartment has a working bathroom, the kids go there every weekend to take baths. One day while waiting for Lori to finish her bath, Jeannette feels Stanley's hand on her thigh. When she looks over, Stanley is masturbating. Jeannette tells Mom, who dismisses the sexual assault as harmless. Unwilling to return to Stanley's, Jeannette stops taking baths.

That spring, heavy rainfall causes flooding all over the county. While the family's house is too high on the hillside to flood, the rain destroys parts of the roof, including above Brian's bed. The moisture also erodes the front steps, causing Mom to fall down the hillside. When people ask about the bruises on her body, she quips, "My husband doesn't beat me. He just won't fix the steps" (185).

Chapters 29-41 Analysis

By the time the Wallses reach Welch, any vestige of adventure left in the family's journey is eliminated from the narrative. There are no cheetah exploits, no stars as Christmas presents, no outdoor pianos. The chapters set in Welch are almost entirely the stuff of American tragedies, as the struggles of the Walls clan in West Virginia resist any efforts to romanticize them. This is in part due to the fact that the family's usual pattern—Dad gets a job, fond memories are forged, Dad loses his job, the family falls into indigence—is largely waylaid here because Dad never even attempts to find steady work.

For the Wallses at least, life in Welch is depicted as truly nightmarish, particularly in comparison to the Southwest. In a simple but telling observation, Jeannette explains why it was easier in Arizona than in Welch to go long periods of time without baths: "We were also always dirty. Not dry-dirty like we'd been in the desert, but grimy-dirty and smudged with oily dust from the coal-burning stove" (140). The relative cleanliness in the desert finds a particularly stark foil in the Tug River and its high levels of fecal matter contamination. Moreover, extreme poverty manifests differently in Welch than it did out West. While Jeannette is no stranger to violence, the violence in Welch is pervasive, cascading on down from overworked miners to their wives to their children to other wives' children. Equally pervasive is racism. Though Jeannette acknowledges that racist attitudes existed toward Mexican and Navajo communities out West, racism is particularly vile and visible in Welch. Multiple characters casually drop racial slurs, and the town is far more segregated than the Wallses' diverse neighborhood in Phoenix.

Jeannette's horrific recollections of the poverty in Welch are supported by the historical record. While the town was a prosperous coal mining community during the first half of the 20th century, a post-World War II shift from coal to oil, combined with greater mechanization of the coal industry, decimated Welch's economic prospects. While Dad is right that the first modern recipients of food stamps received them in Welch, the individual who personally handed them over was in fact Kennedy's Secretary of Agriculture Orville Freeman, not Kennedy himself. Kennedy did visit Welch, only he did so a year earlier as a presidential candidate in the West Virginia primary. A 2014 *New York Times* article reflects on the role in the War on Poverty played by McDowell County, of which Welch is the county seat:

McDowell County, the poorest in West Virginia, has been emblematic of entrenched American poverty for more than a half-century. John F. Kennedy campaigned here in 1960 and was so appalled that he promised to send help if elected president. His first executive order created the modern food stamp program, whose first recipients were McDowell County residents. When President Lyndon B. Johnson declared 'unconditional war on poverty' in 1964, it was the squalor of Appalachia he had in mind. The federal programs that followed—Medicare, Medicaid, free school lunches and others—lifted tens of thousands above a subsistence standard of living. (Gabriel, Trip. "50 Years into the War on Poverty, Poverty Hits Back." *The New York Times*. 20 Apr. 2014. https://www.nytimes.com/2014/04/21/us/50-years-into-the-war-on-poverty-hardship-hits-back.html)

There are some fleeting moments of connection between the characters in Welch, but these connections are generally forged through that same violence that is an ever-present part of life in that community. Consider what Jeannette calls "the Battle of Little Hobart Street" (165), during which Jeannette and Brian heroically conquer their nemesis, Ernie Goad. It is one of the few moments in these chapters when the author musters real excitement in her writing, as she recalls the ingenious mattress catapult she builds with Brian—yet the anecdote ends with a passage that, though exaggerated, highlights the degree to which violence has become an important driving force in the lives of the Walls children: "It was, we were convinced, enough to kill Ernie Goad and his gang, which was what we fully intended to do: kill them and commandeer their bikes, leaving their bodies in the street as a warning to others" (166). Elsewhere, Jeannette details one of the few intimate moments she shares with Dad in Welch, yet it comes as she sews up a deep gash he received earlier in the evening, another act of bonding over violence.

While in Welch, Jeannette is once again in proximity to sexual assault on two occasions: one directly, when Uncle Stanley masturbates while touching her leg, and the other indirectly, when she witnesses Erma molest Brian. This disturbing scene is pivotal in terms of both narrative and character development. From a narrative perspective, it causes the family to be evicted from Erma's basement. In terms of characterization, it reveals the strong likelihood that Dad, too, was a victim of sexual abuse at the hands of Erma. Jeannette recalls her feelings in the wake of the assault:

> It was gross and creepy to think about, but it would explain a lot. Why Dad left home as soon as he could. Why he drank so much and why he got so angry. Why he never wanted to visit Welch when we were younger. Why he at first refused to come to West Virginia with us and only at the last possible moment overcame his reluctance and jumped into the car. Why he was shaking his head so hard, almost like he wanted to put his hands over his ears, when I tried to explain what Erma had been doing to Brian (148).

There is a common saying that people who inflict violence were usually first the victims of violence. While Dad's behavior does not extend to what Erma does to Brian, he has a great deal to answer for in terms of his treatment of Mom and his children, so Jeannette is right: "it would explain a lot" (148). However, the book resists simple explanations for Dad's dysfunction. This logic—that Dad was abused, therefore Dad is an alcoholic, and therefore the family's lives are terrible—is an oversimplification not only of what makes Dad tick, but also of the family's broader relational dynamics.

As for the assault committed by Uncle Stanley, this is one of multiple events in Welch that reveals the extent to which Mom's supposedly progressive ideals crumble when she is faced with necessity and hardship. The other is when Jeannette tells Mom about the racial slurs used by Erma. In both cases, Mom dismisses the events as inconsequential, in large part because she relies on Dad's family to survive. Jeannette recalls, "Situations like these, I realized, were what turned people into hypocrites" (144).

Perhaps the most symbolically rich portions of this section surround the family's first weeks at the dilapidated house on Little Hobart Street. Dad continues to insist that he will build the Glass Castle, and his purchase of the house was driven in large part by the fact that there's enough land on the property to construct it. Moreover, the fact that Jeannette eagerly takes up the task of building a hole for its foundation is evidence that, despite everything, she still hangs onto her innocent childhood illusions about her father. These illusions are cracked—though not yet shattered—when Dad instructs Jeannette to use the foundation of the Glass Castle as a hole for garbage because they cannot afford trash pickup. In essence, Dad wants Jeannette to repurpose the symbolic container for all her hopes and dreams about her father into a literal trashcan. If this symbolic construction occurred in a work of fiction, one might be tempted to call it glaringly, almost comically, obvious, yet this is based on the author's real-life experiences.

In that same chapter, the characters' reactions to improving the exterior of the atrocious-looking house all reflect the innate qualities of each family member. As an optimist, Jeannette tries to paint the house yellow, but the task is too difficult for an 11-year-old, and she ends up making it look worse than before. Mom, habitually more concerned about aesthetics than quality of life, refuses to help because she believes yellow houses look "tacky." As realists or even fatalists, Brian and Lori say they do not have sufficiently sturdy ladders to complete the job. Most tellingly, Dad advises Jeannette not to waste time on projects other than the Glass Castle, once again falling back on an impossible dream to avoid the hard work of real life.

Chapters 42-54

Chapter 42 Summary

Jeannette and Brian find a two-karat diamond ring in a pile of rotting lumber. Rather than sell it for grocery money, Mom insists on keeping it to replace the wedding ring Dad pawned years earlier, adding that self-esteem is more important than food.

In response to Mom's increasingly wild mood swings, Jeannette tells her she needs to leave Dad so she can qualify for welfare. Mom believes that welfare benefits will cause "irreparable psychological damage" to the kids (188). Besides, she adds, she cannot leave Dad, both because she is a Catholic and because she is "an excitement addict" (188).

Chapter 43 Summary

Amid a summer heat wave, Jeannette tries to go to the public pool but is turned away by Ernie Goad and his goons. Later, Dinitia tells Jeannette to come with her to the pool in the morning when the black children swim, in accordance with an unwritten custom of *de facto* segregation in Welch. Struck by the confidence of the other girls, Jeannette changes clothes in the locker room despite the deep shame she feels over her burn scars. At the end of the free swim period, Jeannette recalls, "I'd never felt cleaner" (192).

Chapter 44 Summary

Later that day, a man from child services knocks on the Wallses' door. Neither Mom nor Dad are home, so Jeannette manages to get rid of him before he can see the squalid interior of their home. When Mom returns, Jeannette insists she apply for a teaching job to prevent the state from tearing apart the family. While Mom would rather remain jobless so she has more time to paint and write, Jeannette refuses to take no for an answer. By the end of the week, Mom lands a teaching job 12 miles North of Welch.

Virtually every morning, the kids must drag Mom out of bed and down the hill, where a fellow teacher picks her up for work. At first, the family is able to pay their bills and to buy a few essentials like an electric heater and a refrigerator on layaway, but as the months go on, the money from each paycheck seems to disappear more quickly. Before long, Jeannette is back to rummaging through the trash for food. Mom, meanwhile, manages to buy crystal vases and giant Hershey bars for herself.

Chapter 45 Summary

In the fall, Jeannette enters the seventh grade at Welch High School, a large school filled with other poor kids from all over the area. Although she finds it easier to fit in there, Jeannette laments the fact that none of the boys notice her. She attributes this to her nearly six-foot frame and her massive overbite. In an effort to correct her overbite, Jeannette fashions homemade braces for herself out of rubber bands, a coat hanger, and a sanitary napkin. When

Dad stumbles home one night drunk, he examines the makeshift orthodontics and says, "Those braces are a goddamn feat of engineering genius" (202).

Chapter 46 Summary

Eager to join a club that doesn't require her to pay for an instrument or a uniform, Jeannette joins the school newspaper. She finds a mentor and an ally in faculty advisor Miss Jeannette Bivens, who also taught and supported Dad in high school. When other teachers complain about Jeannette's smell, Bivens vows to fight for her as long as she keeps clean. She resumes her weekend baths at Stanley's apartment despite the threat of another sexual assault. Having realized that writing is not the sole domain of isolated shut-ins like Mom, Jeannette resolves to become a journalist.

Chapter 47 Summary

The following summer, Mom goes to Charleston for two months to take classes to renew her teaching license. With Lori away at a government-funded summer camp for gifted artists, Jeannette is left in charge of the family finances. Mom leaves her $200, or $3.50 a day, on which to survive. At the start of the eight weeks, Jeannette is confident in her ability to prevent Dad from leeching off her, concluding that she is a much stronger woman than Mom. Within two weeks, Dad convinces Jeannette to lend him $30.

The following weekend, Dad tells Jeannette that to pay her back, he needs her to accompany him on a business trip. They stop at a roadside bar, and it becomes clear that Dad's intent is to use Jeannette to help him hustle a man named Robbie at pool. While Robbie flirts with Jeannette, Dad wins $80 off him. Robbie invites Jeannette upstairs, and she worries that he wants something sexual in exchange for losing $80. She expects Dad to intervene, but instead he encourages Jeannette to go with Robbie. Upstairs, Robbie tries to rape Jeannette. He stops only when Jeannette shows him her burn scars and suggests that her entire body is covered with them.

In the car on the ride home, Dad gives Jeannette half of the pool winnings. Instead of being outraged by Robbie's rape attempt, Dad commends Jeannette for successfully resisting the attack. He adds, "It was like that time I threw you into the sulfur spring to teach you to swim" (213).

Chapter 48 Summary

When Jeannette refuses to go out hustling with Dad again, he demands that she stake him $40. A few days later, he steals a $200 oil lease check. Jeannette recalls, "For the first time, I had a clear idea of what Mom was up against" (214). With a month to go before Mom returns and Jeannette running out of money, she gets a $40-a-week job at a jewelry shop.

Chapter 49 Summary

In late August, Mom and Lori return home. To Jeannette, both seem like different people—Lori for the better, and Mom for the worse. Vowing to recommit herself to her art, Mom refuses to get out of bed on the first day of school. Jeannette tells her, "If you want to be treated like a mother, you should act like one" (219). As punishment for back-talking Mom, Dad whips Jeannette with his belt for the first time in years and for the first time ever with anger. From that point forward, Jeannette makes two resolutions: She will never be whipped again, and she will leave Welch before graduating high school.

Chapter 50 Summary

Jeannette and Lori plot their escape. When Lori graduates high school, she will move to New York. After securing a job and a place to stay, Jeannette will follow. The three eldest Walls kids all contribute to an escape fund, which they keep in a piggy bank named Oz—Jeannette by working at the jewelry store and babysitting, Lori by making posters for kids at school, and Brian by mowing lawns.

Chapter 51 Summary

In her efforts to escape New York, Lori faces obstacles at every turn. Her chances of receiving a National Merit Scholarship are dashed when she must hitchhike to Bloomfield to take the test, and a trucker tries to sexually assault her, causing her to botch the exam. She also hopes to win a scholarship on the basis of a sculpture she made of Shakespeare, but Dad—a conspiracy theorist who believes someone else wrote the Bard's plays—destroys it in a drunken fit. Worst of all, Dad steals the escape funds from the piggy bank.

As graduation day looms, one of Jeannette's babysitting clients offers to pay her $200 to accompany the family to Iowa to watch her child for the summer. Jeannette insists that she bring Lori instead and that she buy her a bus ticket to New York as compensation.

Chapter 52 Summary

In tenth grade, Jeannette is made news editor of the school newspaper. Though the two are more estranged than ever, Jeannette and Dad bond briefly when she is assigned to

42

interview Chuck Yeager, a famed test pilot and West
Virginia native who is also Dad's hero.

Chapter 53 Summary

Lori sends Jeannette frequent letters detailing her life in
New York City. She lives in a women's hostel in
Greenwich Village and works at a German restaurant.
Rather than wait until graduation, Jeannette decides to
leave for New York after her junior year. After she tells her
parents, Dad leaves the house without a word, while Mom
appears on the verge of tears. She tells Jeannette, "I'm not
upset because I'll miss you. I'm because you get to go to
New York and I'm stuck here. It's not fair" (237).

A few weeks before her planned departure, Dad asks
Jeannette to look over his old blueprints for the Glass
Castle. As he discusses reworking the layout to account for
Lori's absence, Jeannette tells him, "Dad, you'll never
build the Glass Castle" (238).

Chapter 54 Summary

When Jeannette leaves in the morning to catch her 7:10
a.m. bus, Mom is still asleep. Dad, however, is there on the
front steps and insists on walking her to the bus. As
Jeannette looks out the bus window at her Dad, she thinks
about him leaving Welch at the age of 17, certain he would
never return.

Chapters 42-54 Analysis

Across these chapters, Jeannette's dominant psychological
arc is largely resolved, in that she finally lets go of her
innocent childhood delusions about Dad, as represented by
the symbol of the Glass Castle. There are two important

moments that sever these ties. The first coincides with yet another act of sexual violence committed against Jeannette. The disillusionment comes in waves. For example, when Robbie first begins to flirt with her at the pool hall, she expects Dad to violently intervene. As the night progresses, it becomes clear to Jeannette that she is little more than sexual bait in one of Dad's hustling schemes. Surely Dad won't let Robbie take her upstairs, Jeannette believes—but this, too, transpires without Dad's intervention, leaving Jeannette to rely on her own wits to avoid being raped. This is yet another example of how Mom and Dad's neglect of their children amounts to abuse, in that it forces them into situations in which abuse is likely to occur. Dad may not sexually abuse his children—something worth acknowledging, given his own likely history as a sexual abuse victim—and yet here and elsewhere, his actions indirectly cause such abuse to transpire.

On the ride home, Dad and Jeannette share a telling exchange. Despite the fact that Dad allowed Robbie to flirt with her, to dance with her, and finally to take her upstairs to his room—although she is only around 13—she still holds out hope that Dad will be angry when he discovers Robbie tried to rape her. Instead, he dismisses the attack, adding, "It was like that time I threw you into the sulfur spring to teach you to swim [...] You might have been convinced you were going to drown, but I knew you'd do just fine" (213). By connecting these two traumatic experiences in Jeannette's mind, Dad reveals that his cruelty to her is nothing new, and that the supposedly halcyon days of their relationship—good times aside—were toxic from the start.

This isn't even the betrayal that finally lays Jeannette's illusions about Dad to rest. That comes when Jeannette, after suffering indignity upon indignity at the hands of

Mom and Dad alike, finally stands up for herself and receives a physical beating for it. The beating genuinely shocks her; Dad has whipped his kids in the past, but only when they were children and never with malice. This beating is different, angrier, and in demolishing Jeannette's delusional admiration for Dad, it steels her spirits and empowers her to escape the horrific conditions Mom and Dad created for her and her siblings. Jeannette recalls, "I had been counting on Mom and Dad to get us out, but I now knew I had to do it on my own" (221).

The final confirmation of Jeannette's newfound maturity with respect to her father comes shortly before her departure to New York. As a last-ditch effort to ingratiate himself anew with his daughter, Dad brings out his old blueprints for the Glass Castle. After initially telling him bluntly that he will never build the Glass Castle, Jeannette says, "Dad, as soon as I finish classes, I'm getting on the next bus out of here. If the buses stop running, I'll hitchhike. I'll walk if I have to. Go ahead and build the Glass Castle, but don't do it for me" (238). What neither party says in this moment is that the Glass Castle was never anything more than the increasingly frayed emotional tether between Jeannette and Dad. Once Jeannette cuts that tether and moves on with her life, the Glass Castle is exposed as the illusion it's always been.

Jeannette's relationship with Mom evolves in a less linear manner in these chapters. Mom has long been selfish, and she's long suffered from emotional distress. The incident surrounding the diamond ring, however, suggests that she is seriously psychologically unwell, a possibility that bears out further in the later chapters set in New York. When Jeannette quite reasonably argues that the ring could buy a lot of food, Mom responds, "That's true, but it could also improve my self-esteem. And at times like these, self-esteem is even more vital than food" (186). Moreover, the fact that Mom considers the ring a replacement for the wedding ring Dad sold years ago reflects the extent to which Mom's increasingly incomprehensible behavior is a consequence of her resentment toward Dad.

Conversely, when Jeannette is charged with handling the family's finances in Mom's absence, she comes to empathize with Mom. When Dad steals one of Mom's oil lease checks, Jeannette thinks to herself, "For the first time, I had a clear idea of what Mom was up against. Being a strong woman was harder than I had thought" (214). This is a conclusion reached long ago by Lori, who in these chapters becomes a far more central character. At one point when discussing Mom, Lori references "[p]illars shaped like women. The ones holding up those Greek temples with their heads. I was looking at a picture of some the other day, thinking, Those women have the second toughest job in the world" (208).

Jeannette's newfound empathy for Mom represents personal growth, but it does little to strengthen their relationship. Despite her recognition of Mom's suffering, Jeannette cannot forgive her for quitting her latest teaching job, thus dooming the family once again to indigence. She says, "If you want to be treated like a mother, you should act like one" (219). The events of these chapters with respect to Mom and Dad thus allow Jeannette to achieve maturity along two vectors: empathy and empowerment. This empathy reveals itself once more in Jeannette's final thoughts as her bus drives away from Welch. She recalls, "I wondered if [Dad] was remembering how he, too, had left Welch full of vinegar at age seventeen and just as convinced as I was now that he'd never return" (242). By putting herself in her father's teenage shoes, she tacitly acknowledges how the trauma of his abusive, impoverished upbringing followed him wherever he went, something Jeannette fears might happen to her.

Finally, these chapters further explore the racial dynamics of Welch. Jeannette provides a striking depiction of how *de facto* segregation works when discussing the customs around the local public pool. She writes:

> By 'us' I knew [Dinitia] meant the other black people. The pool was not segregated, anyone could swim at any time—technically, at least—but the fact was that all the black people swam in the morning, when the pool was free, and all the white people swam in the afternoon, when admission was fifty cents. No one had planned this arrangement, and no rules enforced it. That was just the way it was (190).

This passage reveals the extent to which segregation persists as a matter of fact in many parts of the South, long after Supreme Court rulings and civil rights legislation banned the practice in a legal sense. In the process of breaking this taboo and joining Dinitia at the pool, Jeannette experiences what is perhaps the happiest moment of her entire time in Welch, recalling "I'd never felt cleaner" (192). However, she is pressured never to relive this moment by the pervasive bigotry of Welch. Of Dinitia, Jeannette writes, "I guess we both knew that, given the way people in Welch thought about mixing, it would be too weird for us to try to be close friends" (199).

Chapters 55-68

Part 4: "New York City"

Chapter 55 Summary

Jeannette moves in with Lori at the women's hostel and lands a job at a burger joint. A few weeks later, the two of them move into an affordable apartment in the South Bronx. In the fall, Jeannette enrolls at a public school that allows students to take internships rather than attend classes. She obtains an internship at *The Phoenix*, a Brooklyn weekly newspaper run by Mike Armstrong. One day, Mike needs a reporter to cover a zoning board meeting on short notice. Jeannette agrees and is made a full-time reporter at the age of 18.

In letters from Brian, Jeannette reads that Dad is always drunk or in jail, Mom has retreated into her own world, and Maureen is usually at neighbors' houses. Over the phone, Jeannette convinces Brian to move in with her and Lori. The day after he arrives, Brian finds a job at a Brooklyn ice cream shop. Although Jeannette loves her job at *The Phoenix*, Mike convinces her to apply to college. She is accepted to Barnard College. While there, Jeannette lands a job as an editorial assistant at a major magazine. With the situation in Welch deteriorating further, Jeannette convinces Maureen to move in with Lori. Using Brian's new Manhattan address, they enroll Maureen in a Manhattan public school.

Chapter 56 Summary

One morning, Jeannette hears a news report about a broken-down van on the New Jersey Turnpike spilling furniture and clothes all over the road and causing a massive traffic jam. She later learns that the van belongs to Mom and Dad, who arrive in New York that day.

First, Mom and Dad live in a boardinghouse near Lori's apartment, but they are soon evicted for non-payment of rent. They then relocate to a flophouse but are promptly kicked out after Dad accidentally starts a fire. Mom and Dad eventually land in Lori's new apartment, located in the same building where Brian lives. Soon, Lori's apartment is overflowing with Mom's paintings and stacks of street junk. Dad comes home most nights drunk and angry. To alleviate Lori's stress, Brian invites Dad to stay with him, but when Dad breaks off the hinges of Brian's locked liquor cabinet and drinks everything inside, Brian insists that he stop drinking. Dad opts to live in his van instead.

More and more, Dad shows up at Lori's to get into drunken arguments with Mom and the neighbors. Eventually, Lori sees no other option than to kick both Mom and Dad out, a decision Jeannette supports. Mom and Dad live in the van for a few months until the automobile is towed. Jeannette recalls, "That night, they slept on a park bench. They were homeless" (254).

Chapter 57 Summary

Mom and Dad learn to survive on the streets, frequenting soup kitchens and attending free recitals, outdoor concerts, and movie screenings. When Jeannette appeals to Mom to find some other way to live, Mom replies, "Being homeless is an adventure" (255). When the weather cools in the fall, they spend most of their time in libraries. Mom reads Balzac, while Dad reads physics journals.

During a discussion on homelessness in one of Jeannette's classes, she suggests that some people may choose to be homeless. When pressed on the issue by her professor, Jeannette relents rather than share the story of her parents.

Chapter 58 Summary

When the weather turns freezing cold in the winter, Mom's cheerful disposition begins to crack. She refuses to sleep in shelters, so on nights when all the church pews are full, Dad goes to a shelter and Mom comes to Lori's, usually in tears and confessing how hard it is to live on the streets. While Jeannette feels guilty about attending a top university while her parents are homeless, Brian reminds her that Mom still owns property in both Phoenix and Texas, yet she refuses Jeannette's exhortations to sell either property.

Chapter 59 Summary

Mom and Dad make it through the winter, but in the spring, Dad is hospitalized with tuberculosis. When Jeannette visits him, he is sober. Based on his recent research on chaos theory, he says he now believes chaos and turbulence are part of a divine plan. Of his trembling fingers, he explains, "Lack of liquor or fear of God—don't know which is causing it. Maybe both" (261).

Chapter 60 Summary

After a six-week stay in the hospital, Dad is eager to maintain his sobriety by avoiding a return to the streets. Through one of the hospital administrators, Dad lands a maintenance job at a resort upstate with free room and board. Mom refuses to go with him, dismissing Upstate New York as "the sticks." Dad remains there through the summer until November, when Mom convinces him to return to the city. Almost immediately, he starts drinking again.

Meanwhile, Lori is a comic book illustrator, Brian is a warehouse foreman studying to become a police officer, and Maureen is in high school. That Christmas, the whole family gathers at Lori's, where Jeannette gives Dad presents of warm clothes for the winter. Angry and ashamed, Dad puts on his thin bomber jacket and walks out into the cold December air.

Chapter 61 Summary

A month before her last academic year, Jeannette is $1,000 short of her tuition. When Jeannette tells Dad she may have to drop out, he leaves and returns a week later with a brown paper bag full of crumpled bills totaling $950, which he says he earned playing poker.

Chapter 62 Summary

The following month, Mom and Dad move into an abandoned building on the Lower East Side. When Jeannette visits, she is struck by how much their squalid new domicile resembles the house in Welch. Jeannette moves into a Park Avenue apartment with her boyfriend, Eric, a fastidious and independently wealthy small business owner whom she considers the exact opposite of Dad. Of Mom and Dad, she writes, "It seemed as if they had finally found the place where they belonged, and I wondered if I had done the same" (268).

Chapter 63 Summary

Much to Mom's dismay, Jeannette accepts a job writing a weekly column on the lives of New York's elite. Mom asks, "Where are the values I raised you with?" (269). Jeannette loves writing about people who spend as much on a single meal as her parents spent on the house in Welch.

Chapter 64 Summary

Four years after moving in with Eric, Jeannette marries him. Shortly thereafter, Mom asks Jeannette to convince Eric to buy her brother's share of the land they inherited in West Texas, which he plans to sell. She is adamant that the land stay in the family. When Jeannette asks how much the share of land costs, Mom says $1 million and goes on to suggest that her share is worth roughly the same amount.

Jeannette is aghast: "Had all those years, as well as Mom and Dad's time on the street—not to mention their current life in an abandoned tenement—been a caprice inflicted on us by Mom?" (273). Jeannette insists on knowing how much Mom's land is worth, but Mom refuses to entertain the notion of having it appraised.

Chapter 65 Summary

After Maureen graduates, she enrolls in college but eventually drops out and moves in with Mom and Dad. Over time, she retreats into herself, sleeping all day. When Jeannette meets with Maureen to discuss her future, she barely recognizes her younger sister. She suspects she is addicted to drugs.

A few months later, Maureen stabs Mom after an argument over moving out. The police arrest Maureen against Mom's wishes, and a judge sentences her to a psychiatric hospital. Upon her release a year later, Maureen buys a one-way ticket to California and leaves New York without saying goodbye. Jeannette deeply regrets not looking after her more closely.

Chapter 66 Summary

Over the next year, the whole family grows apart. Jeannette almost never sees Mom and Dad. Brian, now a police officer, moves to Long Island with his wife and child.

One day, Dad calls Jeannette to say he needs to talk to her in person, requesting that she bring him a bottle of vodka. Though Jeannette assumes this is little more than a liquor run, she picks up the vodka and heads to his squat. There, Dad reveals he is dying. While Jeannette doesn't believe the absurd yarn he tells about contracting a tropical disease in a fistfight, she believes he is close to death, given the amount of alcohol and cigarettes he consumes. The author writes, "As awful as he could be, I always knew he loved me in a way no one else ever had" (278). After reminiscing for a bit about the Glass Castle and other memories, Jeannette gets up to leave. Dad says, "Hey. Have I ever let you down?" and chuckles (279).

Chapter 67 Summary

Two weeks pass, and Dad suffers a fatal heart attack. A year later, Jeannette divorces Eric. She writes, "He was a good man, but not the right one for me" (280). On clear nights, Jeannette goes out walking and looks for Venus on the horizon.

Part 5: "Thanksgiving"

Chapter 68 Summary

Five years later, Jeannette and her new husband, John, invite Lori, Brian, and Mom to Thanksgiving dinner at their country farmhouse. Mom still lives in the same tenement, except now she occupies it legally thanks to the city's decision to sell each unit to its occupant for a dollar apiece. Over dinner, the family shares favorite memories of Dad, including the cheetah incident and the Christmas when he gave the children stars. Mom raises a glass and toasts to the memory of Dad: "Life with your father was never boring" (288), she says.

Chapters 55-68 Analysis

More than perhaps anywhere else, Part 4 examines the motivations underlying Mom's lifestyle and character. Perhaps this is because Jeannette, as a narrator, is finally an adult who is better capable of taking stock of what individuates Mom. Or perhaps, now that Mom no longer has a family to take care of, we can better view her character without the context and expectations of her responsibilities as a mother. Even still, Jeannette is if anything more perplexed than ever by her mother, particularly after she learns that Mom owns land worth a million dollars. Jeannette recalls:

> I was thunderstruck. All those years in Welch with no food, no coal, no plumbing, and Mom had been sitting on land worth a million dollars? Had all those years, as well as Mom and Dad's time on the street—not to mention their current life in an abandoned tenement—been a caprice inflicted on us by Mom? (273).

This revelation further complicates Mom's role in causing the family's transient, impoverished conditions over the years. Throughout much of the book, Dad tends to bear the lion's share of the blame for their circumstances. For all his treachery and cruelty, Jeannette could see some of the factors behind his dysfunction. He was abused. He's an alcoholic. The discovery that Mom is in possession of roughly a million dollars in assets renders their entire upbringing incomprehensibly pointless. It also calls into question whether Mom is not simply an enabler stuck in a toxic codependent relationship with Dad; she may be seriously unwell herself.

Moreover, that toxic codependence works both ways. When Dad briefly relocates upstate following his hospitalization and newfound sobriety, it is Mom who convinces him to return to New York City, where he is sure to fall back into his old drinking habits. Jeannette is careful not to judge either party individually in this, acknowledging instead her parents' codependent relationship by quoting Dad as saying, "This crazy-ass mother of yours, can't live with her, can't live without her. And damned if she doesn't feel the same about me" (262).

The closest Jeannette comes to settling on a unified theory of Mom and Dad's philosophy of life comes when she visits them for the first time at their abandoned tenement, which bears a disturbing resemblance to their old house on Little Hobart Street. She recalls, "[I]t became clear they'd stumbled on an entire community of people like themselves, people who lived unruly lives battling authority and who liked it that way. After all those years of roaming, they'd finally found home" (267). At the same time, Jeannette is ambivalent concerning the extent to which her parents' lifestyle is an active choice. For example, in the class discussion on homelessness, Jeannette argues that some people—specifically her parents—do not fit into either the left-wing or the right-wing theory of poverty. In other words, they are neither victims of too much government nor victims of too little government, and instead they "get the lives they want" (256). She quickly backtracks on this claim, concluding, "I just didn't have it in me to argue Mom and Dad's case to the world" (256).

Maureen's fate is also covered in the final chapters. Considering the upbringing of the four Walls children, one might find it surprising that only one succumbs to mental illness and possible drug abuse. However, it may be less surprising that of the four, Maureen would be the one to suffer most in adulthood. The three eldest children were all closer in age, and the bonds they forged between them guided them through the worst years of their childhood. Maureen, however, was always an outsider, relying on the charity of neighbors as opposed to the potentially deeper bonds of her siblings. When recounting the moment of Maureen's birth, Jeannette writes, "I promised her I'd always take care of her" (46). It is this broken promise she likely has in mind when Jeannette, finally reunited with Maureen under undisclosed circumstances, says, "I'm sorry, Maureen, sorry for everything" (276). Indeed, every member of the Walls clan ends up failing to provide the proper support for its youngest and most vulnerable member, which is perhaps why, according to Jeannette, "Something in all of us broke [on the day of Maureen's arraignment], and afterward, we no longer had the spirit for family gatherings" (277).

Finally, the motif of turbulence and order is revisited, once in Part 4 and a second time in Part 5. As Dad recovers from both tuberculosis and alcohol withdrawal, he quotes the physicist Mitchell Feigenbaum, who helped pioneer the field of chaos theory. Jeannette writes, "Dad said he was damned if Feigenbaum didn't make a persuasive case that turbulence was not in fact random but followed a sequential spectrum of varying frequencies" (261). In other words, chaos conforms to a rational pattern. Dad's takeaway from this is that it implies the existence of God. It may also, however, suggest that the chaos that Mom and Dad inflicted on the family is part of some divine plan. This is an uncomfortable conclusion, given the very real suffering that could have been avoided at so many turns had Mom and Dad made different choices. Once again, the extent to which choice is a factor in the Wallses' circumstances is a question the author leaves somewhat open to interpretation.

It may be that Walls prefers to punt on the question of personal responsibility because it makes it easier for her to forgive Dad and to focus on the good memories she shared with him rather than the bad. This approach stands in contrast to Dad's inability to reconcile the trauma caused by Erma, which may explain why, far from causing him relief, her death results in a further spiral into agony and depression. In any case, it is notable that the book ends with a remembrance of Dad's good qualities and the happier memories the family shared with him, followed by one last reference to chaos. In a final tribute to Dad, the author ends with the lines, "A wind picked up, rattling the windows, and the candle flames suddenly shifted, dancing along the border between turbulence and order" (288).

Jeannette Walls

The narrator and protagonist of the book, Jeannette Walls is an American author and journalist. Born in 1960 in Phoenix, Arizona, Walls is the second of four children raised by Rex and Rose Mary Walls, whom she refers to throughout the book as Mom and Dad. Her earliest memory is of suffering severe burns at the age of three after being left alone to cook hot dogs unsupervised. She has red hair, and she describes herself as having been nearly six feet tall as a teenager with a massive overbite that she attempted to correct with homemade braces.

Jeannette's primary psychological arc in the book involves a process of letting go of her childhood illusions about Dad, which are represented symbolically by his plans to build a sustainable Glass Castle where the family will live. These illusions erode bit by bit as the family's situation deteriorates. Even after their move to the dilapidated house on Little Hobart Street, Jeannette continues to have faith in the Glass Castle and, by extension, her father. This faith suffers a serious blow when Dad insists that Jeannette use the foundation she and Brian dug for the Glass Castle as a hole for the family's garbage. Jeannette's admiration for Dad is irreparably damaged when, around the age of 13, Dad uses her as sexual bait in one of his pool hustling schemes and she must fight off a would-be rapist. She finally lets go of her increasingly toxic attachment to Dad after he whips her with his belt following a fight.

At the end of Jeannette's junior year in high school, she moves in with her sister Lori in New York. She spends her senior year working at the newspaper *The Phoenix* and receives a scholarship to attend Barnard College to study journalism. She goes on to write a gossip column for *Esquire* Magazine, leading her mother to ask, "Where are the values I raised you with?" (269). Indeed, Jeannette is torn about living in luxury with her wealthy husband while her Mom and Dad are either homeless or living in squalor in an abandoned tenement. In the end, however, Jeannette comes to grips with the fact that, regardless of her parents' mistakes and regardless of whether they truly choose to live the way they do, they "stumbled on an entire community of people like themselves, people who lived unruly lives battling authority and who liked it that way" (267).

Dad

Rex Walls, referred to in the book as Dad, is the patriarch of the Walls clan. He is tall, handsome, intelligent, and charming, yet he is also constantly undone by his increasingly debilitating alcoholism, which exacerbates his natural tendencies toward paranoia and stubbornness. Like Mom, he is intensely distrustful of authority. He prefers a self-sufficient lifestyle as far away as possible from the levers of civil power. These preferences are embodied by his plans to build a solar-powered Glass Castle that would allow him and the rest of the Wallses to live entirely off the grid.

At the beginning of the book, Dad's alcoholism is severe but not entirely unmanageable. He tends to repeat a similar pattern each time he brings his family to a new town: He gets a job, things are stable for a period of months or weeks, he loses his job under circumstances that are generally vague to the narrator, and then he spirals deeper into alcoholism, disappearing for days at a time until the family moves on to another community. He is fixated on turbulence, order, and the boundary in-between, where he says "no rules apply" (61). Dad's life seems to be in a state of near-constant chaos, and every time he begins to teeter across the boundary into order, he sabotages himself and, by extension, his family.

When Dad's mother, Erma, molests Brian, Dad angrily refuses to believe it. Jeannette wonders if Dad, too, was a victim of sexual abuse at the hands of Erma. Jeannette concludes, "It would explain a lot" (148), and indeed, Dad displays a number of symptoms associated with childhood trauma, including a need to self-medicate and severe anger issues, particularly when he drinks. That said, even at his worst moments, he is capable of genuine affection, particularly toward Jeannette, though these moments are fewer and less frequent as the book progresses.

At the age of 59, after years of heavy drinking and smoking, Dad suffers a fatal heart attack while living in an abandoned New York City tenement with Mom.

Mom

Rose Mary Walls, referred to by the narrator as Mom, is Rex's wife and mother to Lori, Jeannette, Brian, and Maureen. She was raised in Texas by her wealthy mother, Grandma Smith. Little is revealed about Mom's relationship with her own mother except that Mom deeply resents her and strives to raise Jeannette and the other Walls children with very few restrictions or rules as a rebuke to Grandma Smith. A lifelong artist with major ambitions, Mom also resents Grandma Smith for all but forcing her to obtain a teaching degree to fall back on should her art career fail. For that reason, Mom is deeply reluctant to pick up teaching jobs, even when the family is penniless. She married Dad only when he refused to take no for an answer, and primarily to escape her own mother.

She later tells Jeannette, "I had no idea your father would be even worse" (27).

Throughout the book, Mom displays codependent behavior with respect to Dad's alcoholism. She is tolerant of the squalor and chaos he brings into their lives if it means she can spend her days painting and writing without any additional responsibilities. Early on in the book, Mom romanticizes this chaos as a reflection of the family's indomitable sense of adventure. Whenever Dad displays especially severe cruelty or neglect, she tends to dismiss this behavior, adding that she is "an excitement addict" (188). She rarely nurtures her children, justifying this treatment with a belief that struggle makes children stronger and more beautiful, a notion symbolized by the Joshua trees she loves to paint.

After moving to Welch, however, Mom's sanguine attitude toward life begins to erode. As their circumstances worsen and Dad continues to spiral into ever-deeper levels of alcoholism, she suffers wild mood swings. When she finally submits to Jeannette's demand that she obtain a teaching job, she spends a disproportionate amount of her paycheck on luxury items like crystal vases, insisting that "self-esteem is more vital than food" (186).

Of all the characters' behavior, Mom's may be the most incomprehensible to Jeannette. For example, it is revealed late in the book that Mom owns a tract of oil land in Texas worth $1 million but refuses to sell it, despite the fact that she could have lifted herself and her children out of starvation-level poverty.

Lori Walls

The eldest Walls child, Lori is roughly three years older than Jeannette. She is the one child who seems to have a close relationship with Mom, though the exact details of this relationship are often a mystery to Jeannette, much as the details of Jeannette's relationship with Dad are likely a mystery to Lori. Because of the age gap, Jeannette is much less close with Lori than she is with Brian during their childhood. This relationship changes once Jeannette reaches high school and proves to be instrumental in facilitating Lori's move to New York. There, Lori follows in her mother's footsteps to become an artist, albeit one who is gainfully employed as an illustrator of comic books. When Mom and Dad move to New York, Lori initially opens up her home to them, but before long she is forced to evict them, a decision Jeannette supports. At the end of the book, it is suggested that Lori and Mom are still fairly close, as they arrive together to Jeannette's Thanksgiving dinner.

Brian Walls

Brian is Jeannette's younger brother and her primary ally as they struggle to survive the family's harsh circumstances. Though less intellectual than Jeannette or Lori, Brian is capable and loyal, particularly to Jeannette. Brian and Jeannette constantly look out for one another, both in childhood and in New York as young adults. Unlike Jeannette, Brian becomes disillusioned with Dad fairly early on after an incident in which Dad makes him wait outside the bedroom door on his birthday while he has sex with a woman from the Green Lantern. In adulthood, Brian becomes a police officer and has a daughter with his wife, whom he later divorces.

Maureen Walls

The youngest of the Walls, Maureen is around four years younger than Jeannette. In part because of this age gap, she never builds the kind of strong sibling bonds that hold Jeannette, Brian, and Lori together. For much of the family's time in Welch, Maureen is fed and cared for by various neighbors whose sons and daughters she befriends. She, too, relocates to New York City, but she has a far more difficult time adjusting than the rest of her siblings. After dropping out of college, she moves in with Mom and Dad in their abandoned tenement and retreats inward. The breadth of her psychological problems comes to the fore when she stabs Mom following an intense argument. Maureen is sent to a psychiatric hospital upstate for a year, and upon her release she moves to California without saying goodbye to the rest of the family.

Letting Go of Childhood Illusions

The dominant psychological arc of *The Glass Castle* is Jeannette's slow yet certain rejection of her illusions concerning Dad. For much of her early childhood, Jeannette believes "Dad was perfect" (23). His intelligence, his sense of humor, and perhaps most of all his ambitions to build the Glass Castle place Dad upon a pedestal in Jeannette's mind. Her love of her father may also stem from the fact that, superficially at least, he is far more nurturing than Mom.

These illusions, however, begin to fall away along two vectors: Jeannette's growing personal maturity and the worsening conditions of her life with Dad. Perhaps the earliest incident that threatens Jeannette's admiration for Dad comes when she falls out of the Green Caboose on the way to Las Vegas and an intoxicated Dad drives for miles before retrieving her. Significantly injured both physically and emotionally, Jeannette initially resists Dad's attempts to comfort her, but all is forgiven when Dad tells her, "Damn, honey. You busted your snot locker pretty good" (31), causing her to convulse in fits of laughter. Just as Dad's charm allows him to ingratiate himself with prospective employers on numerous occasions, his sense of humor tends to paper over intentional and unintentional acts of abuse and neglect. Consider, too, the year the family cannot afford even discounted secondhand Christmas presents for the kids. Rather than lament these circumstances, Jeannette feels lucky to receive the planet Venus from Dad for Christmas as opposed to cheap store-bought toys. Here and elsewhere early in the book, Dad finds ways to perpetuate Jeannette's illusions about his qualities as a father by framing their transience and poverty as a grandiose adventure.

These illusions are further threatened by the Hot Pot incident, in which Dad repeatedly heaves Jeannette into stinking, sulfuric water to teach her to swim. In the moment, his behavior angers Jeannette to no end, yet when Dad tells her he did it for her own good, she accepts his reasoning without question. Jeannette recalls, "Once I got my breath back, I figured he must be right. There was no other way to explain it" (66). Of course, there are plenty of other ways to explain it—cruelty, recklessness, all-purpose bad parenting—but Jeannette is not yet ready to accept that her long-held attitudes about Dad are based on a delusion.

During this same period of her childhood, Jeannette's attitudes about Dad are contrasted with those of her brother, Brian. Brian far more readily rejects any delusional notions he may have had about Dad after the incident with Ginger, when Dad not only uses Brian's birthday excursion as an excuse to have an affair with a sex worker, but also gives Brian's birthday present to her. Given this betrayal, Brian is able to look on Dad with clear eyes far earlier than Jeannette is.

Once the family relocates to Welch, Jeannette's illusions become increasingly difficult to maintain. A series of betrayals transpire, the first of which is largely symbolic. With Dad increasingly absent, Jeannette entertains her illusions concerning him by digging a foundation for the Glass Castle. As the garbage piles up inside the Little Hobart house, Dad orders Jeannette to use the foundation as a hole for their garbage. Even an adolescent like Jeannette can surely sense the symbolism of the Glass Castle being turned into a literal garbage can—yet even then, Jeannette clings to her admiration for her father, not necessarily for any logical reasons but because to acknowledge her illusions would mean calling into question all the times she assumed he was acting out of love.

Clinging to these illusions becomes impossible, however, after the incident at the roadside bar. Dad willingly puts his daughter in harm's way, causing her to nearly be raped, and all for $80. As if this betrayal isn't enough, Dad connects it to the earlier Hot Pot incident, telling her, "It was like that time I threw you into the sulfur spring to teach you to swim […] You might have been convinced you were going to drown, but I knew you'd do just fine" (213). To Jeannette, it is without question that their present relationship is deeply toxic. This admission reveals that their relationship, despite sporadic moments of joy, has always been toxic.

The Reasons and Motivations Behind Mom and Dad's Lifestyle

Some of the most intractable questions posed by *The Glass Castle* involve why Mom and Dad, despite being skilled, able-bodied individuals, repeatedly make choices that lead to a life of indigence for themselves and their children. To think of Mom and Dad's vagrant lifestyle and later homelessness as a choice is an uncomfortable conclusion to reach—particularly for liberal-minded individuals like Jeannette—but particularly following the revelation that Mom owns land worth $1 million, it is difficult to view her poverty as anything other than a conscious decision.

That said, there are other circumstances to consider, the most obvious of which is Dad's alcoholism. If one follows the lead of mainstream mental health doctrine and considers alcoholism to be a disease, this circumstance certainly complicates the narrative that Dad's dysfunction is entirely his fault. Jeannette also strongly suggests that

Dad is a survivor of sexual abuse, and self-medication through drugs and alcohol is often a long-term symptom of childhood trauma. At the same time, there are clearly broader philosophical factors at play, as both parents are intensely anti-conformist and distrustful of authority. However, philosophy alone cannot account for Mom and Dad's lifestyle. Rather, their circumstances seem to be the result of a perfect storm that includes trauma, substance abuse, quirks of personality and philosophy, and perhaps mental illness, though Jeannette is careful not to attempt to diagnose either parent in this respect.

Indeed, it may at times feel frustrating to the reader that the author fails to provide much in the way of answers as to why Mom and Dad behave the way they do. In a work of fiction, this lack of answers could be problematic. This book, however, is a memoir about real people, whose motivations are often far too difficult to process, even by the people closest to them and even by themselves.

The Destructiveness of Codependent Relationships

Dad's alcoholism and Mom's attempts to cope with it present an instructive case study in codependent relationships. Broadly speaking, codependency involves a person who enables a partner's self-destructive behavior because of his or her own psychological traits and the dynamics of the relationship between the two. As a devoted artist who is willing to live in squalor if it means she can work on her art all day, Mom often fails to put pressure on Dad to get a job rather than drink at the bar all day. In fact, it is usually when Mom herself has to get a job—and is thus deprived of the opportunity to concentrate on art—that her anger toward Dad bubbles over.

One of the clearest manifestations of her toxic codependent relationship with Dad comes when Mom tells the kids not to clean up after his most recent drunken rampage. She says, "Your father needs to see the mess he's making of our lives" (112). Because Dad knows that Mom has an extraordinarily high tolerance for squalor, he has no real reason to clean up the mess himself, nor to stop engaging in the behavior that causes these destructive episodes in the first place. Under normal circumstances, cleaning up after Dad would be the behavior of an enabler, but these are not normal circumstances. Furthermore, even at her lowest points, Mom observes the wreckage of her life through the lens of adventure and excitement—a coping mechanism that enables Dad to continue hurling the family into ever deeper states of chaos.

An even clearer example of enabling comes when Dad quits drinking and moves upstate to work at a resort. Mom refuses to join him, but Dad realizes that if he returns to the city, he will start drinking again, in part because the city is full of familiar triggers and in part because life there is so full of hardship. Eventually, however, Mom, lonely for his presence, wears him down and convinces him to return, whereupon he immediately starts drinking again. Mom may be a victim of a toxic, verbally abusive relationship with Dad, but her tolerance for chaos and her addiction to excitement feed into and exacerbate Dad's self-destructive tendencies.

How Poverty Increases the Likelihood of Abuse

The events of this book call into question the extent to which Mom and Dad could be characterized as "abusive" parents. Dad does dole out physical punishment, not uncommon in the 1960s, and Walls adopts a rather sanguine attitude toward this punishment, writing, "Dad whipped us with his belt, but never out of anger, and only if we back-talked or disobeyed a direct order, which was rare" (59). At least for Jeannette, however, the more traumatic abuse she suffers is more indirect, arriving through neglect. When two able-bodied and intellectually capable parents like Mom and Dad fail to provide food for their children, this, too, may be seen as a form of abuse. Moreover, Mom pithily addresses the relationship between abuse and neglect after she falls through the front steps and suffers extensive bruising. She tells the neighbors, "My husband doesn't beat me. He just won't fix the steps" (185).

There is another class of abuse the Walls children endure, however, not at the direct hands of Mom or Dad but indirectly, arising out of the conditions in which they live. For example, if Mom and Dad could afford a house with running water, Jeannette would not need to bathe at her grandfather's house, where she becomes the victim of sexual abuse by Uncle Stanley. The family's circumstances also force Lori to hitchhike to her National Merit Scholarship test and suffer the pawing and verbal predations of a trucker. Most explicitly, Dad knowingly places Jeannette in a situation in which she is likely to be raped by Robbie. In fact, the only reason she isn't raped is that she manages to outwit her would-be assailant.

Jeannette observes how poverty causes violence and abuse outside her own family as well. Commenting on the cascades of violence in Welch, Walls says that poor, overworked miners "came home and took it out on their wives, who took it out on their kids, who took it out on other kids" (164).

The Glass Castle

The Glass Castle is an imagined solar-powered house made entirely of glass that Dad vows to build once he has enough money. It operates as an important symbol on two levels. On the first level, it represents Dad's ideal life: sustainable, self-sufficient, and not reliant on any larger authority. For Jeannette, however, the symbolism runs deeper. The Glass Castle comes to stand in for all her hopes and dreams concerning her father. He may be an alcoholic, he may be woefully underemployed, and he may be destructive and cruel at turns, but as long as he still plans to build the Glass Castle, he has the potential to be the kind of loving provider she long expects him to become.

Over the course of the book, this illusion falls apart. One particularly dramatic erosion of Jeannette's hope in her father comes when Dad tells her to throw their mounting garbage piles into the hole she dug for the Glass Castle's foundation. Over time, the Glass Castle comes to symbolize failure for Jeannette, while for Dad it comes to represent his preference for dreaming up impossible projects in lieu of doing the hard work of lifting his family out of poverty. It also represents an increasingly frayed emotional tether connecting Jeannette and Dad, one that is severed permanently when Jeannette decides to leave Welch. She tells him, "Go ahead and build the Glass Castle, but don't do it for me" (238).

Turbulence and Order

When Dad describes the heat emanating from the tops of the flames of the shack Jeannette and Brian set on fire, he characterizes it creating a boundary between turbulence and order. The concepts of turbulence, order, and the space in-between provide an instructive lens through which to consider the lives of the Walls family, and particularly Dad's life. Given that Dad is more comfortable with chaos, whenever the family succeeds enough to come into proximity with stability—that is, to exist within that boundary between turbulence and order—Dad finds a way to sabotage it.

The scene at the zoo when Dad pets the cheetah and invites Jeannette to do the same is another moment of high adventure that nevertheless exists in that space between turbulence and order that is dangerous for the Walls. Finally, Jeannette recalls her Dad's musings at the burning shack in the final line of the novel, writing, "A wind picked up, rattling the windows, and the candle flames suddenly shifted, dancing along the border between turbulence and order" (288).

Christmas

Over the course of the novel, Christmas tends to reveal a great deal about the dynamics of the Walls family. For example, the Christmas in the desert when Dad gives Jeannette the planet Venus because he cannot afford store-bought presents reveals the extent to which life still feels like a grandiose adventure for the Walls. Moreover, it shows that Dad is still able to present their lack of means in a way that charms and delights Jeannette. By contrast, the disastrous Christmas in Phoenix, when Dad destroys the tree and the presents during a drunken rampage, reflects the utter chaos threatening to destroy the Walls family if Dad does not make major changes. Finally, the Christmas in New York when Jeannette shames her father by giving him warm clothes reflects how the children's fortunes have transcended those of Mom and Dad, emphasizing to Dad his failure as a provider.

The Joshua Tree

While driving through the mountains of California, Mom stops to paint an ancient Joshua tree. To Jeannette, the tree is ugly, stuck in a "permanent state of windblownness" (35). However, when Jeannette finds a Joshua tree sapling and vows to protect it from the wind so it grows tall and straight, Mom chastises her, saying, "You'd be destroying what makes it special. [...] It's the Joshua tree's struggle that gives it its beauty" (38). This is but one of many ways Mom fetishizes struggle and uses it to justify her unwillingness to better nurture her children.

1. "I was sitting in a taxi, wondering if I had overdressed for the evening, when I looked out the window and saw Mom rooting through a Dumpster." (Chapter 1, Page 3)

   In these opening lines, the author paints a picture full of stark contrasts. Jeanette worries about such trivial matters as whether her stylish clothes are appropriate for the evening at hand, while her homeless Mom struggles to find dinner from other people's refuse. The quote also foreshadows the complicated feelings of guilt and shame Jeannette feels when she takes stock of her own success in light of the squalor in which her parents live.

2. "That was the thing about the hospital. You never had to worry about running out of stuff like food or ice or even chewing gum. I would have been happy staying in that hospital forever." (Chapter 2, Page 12)

   Little is known about the Wallses' life at this point in the book. However, the fact that Jeannette would rather live in the hospital than return to her life in the trailer park speaks volumes about the struggles her family faces. It also renders Dad's late-night abduction of Jeannette from the hospital all the more symbolic, as he rips her from a state of existence in which all her needs are addressed.

3. "The next day the saguaros and prickly pears were fat from drinking as much as they could, because they knew it might be a long, long time until the next rain. We were sort of like the cactus. We ate irregularly, and when we did, we'd gorge ourselves." (Chapter 5, Page 22)

The extent to which the Wallses are well-suited to desert life is illustrated here, with the saguaros and prickly pears standing in as symbols for their hunger. Mom in particular would appreciate this symbolism, given her insistence that beauty is forged through struggle and therefore desert landscapes are most beautiful. That said, the book regularly calls into question whether Mom truly has her children's best interests in mind when it comes to her approach toward parenting, or whether her aphorisms are merely excuses to justify her inability or refusal to nurture her children.

4. "That was why we had to find gold. To get Mom a new wedding ring. That and so we could build the Glass Castle." (Chapter 6, Page 28)

   This comes shortly after the first mention of the Glass Castle, the dominant symbol in the book. The Glass Castle represents an impossible dream that nevertheless helps the characters maintain a sense of hope for the future. Juxtaposing the impossible Glass Castle with what is frankly an achievable goal—getting Mom a new wedding ring—highlights the extent to which Dad cannot be relied upon for even the most modest achievements. In other words, the chances of Dad working in one place long enough to save up for a new wedding ring are roughly equal to his chances of building an impossible house made entirely of glass.

5. "I wondered if the fire had been out to get me. I wondered if all fire was related, like Dad said all humans were related, if the fire that had burned me that day while I cooked hot dogs was somehow connected to the fire I had flushed down the toilet and the fire burning at the hotel. I didn't have the answers to those

questions, but what I did know was that I lived in a world that at any moment could erupt into fire. It was the sort of knowledge that kept you on your toes." (Chapter 8, Page 34)

At the start of the book, danger and excitement go hand in hand for Jeannette. Despite almost dying twice as a result of fire, Jeannette views fire a unified symbol for everything that keeps life with Mom and Dad interesting. It is only when she grows older that she comes to realize allowing your three-year-old child to use the stove unsupervised or leaving that same child alone in a flophouse with a book of matches for an hour doesn't constitute the makings of a great adventure. It's simply neglect.

6. "One time I saw a tiny Joshua tree sapling growing not too far from the old tree. I wanted to dig it up and replant it near our house. I told Mom that I would protect it from the wind and water it every day so that it could grow nice and tall and straight. Mom frowned at me. 'You'd be destroying what makes it special,' she said. 'It's the Joshua tree's struggle that gives it its beauty.'" (Chapter 9, Page 38)

Like the saguaro and the prickly pear, the Joshua tree is a powerful symbol for how Mom views her children. To Jeannette, the dry and windblown Joshua tree is a symbol of ugliness and neglect. Why not nurture it, Jeannette wonders, so it can grow tall and proud like other trees. Mom's response reflects two important aspects of her character. The first is that she romanticizes hardship, in part as a coping mechanism to help her survive her chaotic life with Dad. The second is that, as an artist, Mom tends to view everything in abstract, aesthetic terms, often to the detriment of her children's well-being.

7. "We laughed about all the kids who believed in the Santa myth and got nothing for Christmas but a bunch of cheap plastic toys. 'Years from now, when all the junk they got is broken and long forgotten,' Dad said, 'you'll still have your stars.'" (Chapter 10, Page 41)

This quote serves a number of purposes, the first of which is to introduce Christmas as a dominant motif that reflects the family's dynamic in a given year. This Christmas season, when Dad gives stars and a planet to the children because he cannot afford store-bought gifts, represents the life of the Walls at its most romantic. They have nothing but each other, but in this moment, that is enough. In fact, it is more than enough, at least to Jeannette, who views her family's differences as a badge of honor. As Jeannette grows older and the family sinks deeper into poverty, this heavily romanticized view of her father will fade.

8. "My favorite rocks to find were geodes, which Mom said came from the volcanoes that had erupted to form the Tuscarora Mountains millions of years ago, during the Miocene period. From the outside, geodes looked like boring round rocks, but when you broke them open with a chisel and hammer, the insides were hollow, like a cave, and the walls were covered with glittering white quartz crystals or sparkling purple amethysts." (Chapter 15, Page 60)

Unlike her mother, Jeannette is not terribly concerned with aesthetics or appearances. Perhaps this lack of concern is due to her own insecurities about the way she looks, in part a consequence of the severe scarring on her legs from the cooking accident. Thus, the geode symbolizes her inner beauty—a perhaps obvious metaphor for Jeannette herself, yet also a powerful one, given that for much of her life as a child, she assesses her own value based on Dad's repeated acknowledgement of the beauty that exists inside her. The geode is in many ways the opposite of the Joshua tree, which reflects its beauty outward.

9. "Then he pointed to the top of the fire, where the snapping yellow flames dissolved into an invisible shimmery heat that made the desert beyond seem to waver, like a mirage. Dad told us that zone was known in physics as the boundary between turbulence and order. 'It's a place where no rules apply, or at least they haven't figured 'em out yet,' he said. 'You-all got a little too close to it today.'" (Chapter 15, Page 61)

Turbulence and order are major fixations for Dad, whose own life seems to constantly teeter in that dangerous space between these two states. Despite his warning, Dad seems most comfortable existing within this boundary, given his tendency to vacillate between order and chaos in his own life. The author, however, characterizes this zone as a mirage. Indeed, whatever happiness or fulfillment Dad achieves by positioning himself at the nexus of order and turbulence is largely illusory.

10. "Dad kept telling me that he loved me, that he never would have let me drown, but you can't cling to the side your whole life, that one lesson every parent needs to teach a child is 'If you don't want to sink, you better figure out how to swim.' What other reason, he asked, would possibly make him do this? Once I got my breath

back, I figured he must be right. There was no other way to explain it." (Chapter 17, Page 66)

The book's chief psychological arc concerns Jeannette's passage into adulthood by letting go of her illusions about Dad. This is one of the earliest instances in which Jeannette questions whether Dad truly cares about her well-being. However, at this point in the book, Jeannette is not ready to acknowledge Dad's capacity for abuse and cruelty, nor is she ready to see the more toxic elements of their relationship with clear eyes.

11. "I hated Billy at that moment, I really did. I thought of telling him about binary numbers and the Glass Castle and Venus and all the things that made my dad special and completely different from his dad, but I knew Billy wouldn't understand. I started to run out of the house, but then I stopped and turned around. 'My daddy is nothing like your daddy!' I shouted. 'When my daddy passes out, he never pisses himself!'" (Chapter 21, Page 83)

This quote effectively captures Jeannette's rather delusional attitude toward her father. She is perfectly willing to accept that Dad is a drunk, but the fact that he is able to pass out without urinating himself elevates him to a hero's status in her mind. Furthermore, her outburst of anger against Billy suggests a great deal of repressed anger toward her own father, which she fails to acknowledge so as to maintain her delusions.

12. "'I'm not so sure,' Dad said. 'Every damn thing in the universe can be broken down into smaller things, even atoms, even protons, so theoretically speaking, I guess you had a winning case. A collection of things should

be considered one thing. Unfortunately, theory don't always carry the day.'" (Chapter 23, Page 99)

This quote comes in response to Jeannette's insistence that she should have been able to take her entire rock collection to Phoenix and not just one geode. Dad prohibits the children from taking more than one favored object every time they move, perhaps as an effort to discourage an overreliance on material objects. There's also a deeper subtext to this quote. As an enthusiast of physics, Dad overwhelmingly relies on theoretical notions in his everyday life, stubbornly resisting anything he might perceive as conformity or authority. If he were willing to be more flexible with respect to these theoretical concepts, he would be far better-suited to provide for his family.

13. "I could hear people around us whispering about the crazy drunk man and his dirty little urchin children, but who cared what they thought? None of them had ever had their hand licked by a cheetah." (Chapter 25, Page 109)

Until now, almost every observation of the Walls family is filtered through Jeannette's childhood perspective and thus informed by a series of illusions she holds dear. Only here does the reader hear how the Wallses are perceived from the outside, as "dirty little urchin children" with their "crazy drunk" father. For Jeannette, filth and drunkenness are normalized and therefore rarely addressed in these terms. This quote also serves a second function: to reflect how Jeannette, at this point in the book, still tries to justify her family's hardship by pointing out that without her Dad's unfettered devotion to chaos, she would have never had the singular experience of being licked by a cheetah.

14. "She'd been reading books on how to cope with an alcoholic, and they said that drunks didn't remember their rampages, so if you cleaned up after them, they'd think nothing had happened. 'Your father needs to see the mess he's making of lives,' Mom said. But when Dad got up, he'd act as if all the wreckage didn't exist, and no one discussed it with him." (Chapter 26, Page 112)

This is a stark example of Mom's codependent behavior with respect to Dad. The advice she shares is valid under normal circumstances, and her efforts to address Dad's alcoholism are admirable. However, because Mom has already shown so much tolerance for chaos and squalor, Dad does not think twice about waking up amid the wreckage of his latest drunken rampage. So while up after an alcoholic partner is an act of enabling, in this scenario, Mom's refusal to clean up after Dad is equally enabling.

15. "But Dad said 93 Little Hobart Street was such a dump that we shouldn't waste time or energy on it that we could be devoting to the Glass Castle. Mom said she thought bright yellow houses were tacky. Brian and Lori said we didn't have the ladders and scaffolding we needed." (Chapter 35, Page 157)

Each character's response to Jeannette's efforts to beautify the house on Little Hobart Street reflects their character. Mom, for example, views virtually everything—including potential acts of self-improvement—through aesthetic terms. Brian and Lori have come to adopt a fatalistic attitude toward their circumstances. Finally, Dad continues to focus on impossible dreams like the Glass Castle, rather than accomplish smaller, achievable goals like painting the house they already have.

16. "His face was tight and closed, but I could tell he was distraught. More distraught than I'd ever seen him, which surprised me, because Erma had seemed to have some sort of an evil hold over Dad, and I thought he'd be relieved to be free of it." (Chapter 41, Page 180)

    While the logic that Dad would be happy to be rid of his abuser is sound to Jeannette, it also reflects a child's understanding of trauma. As shown through Dad's reaction to Brian's sexual abuse at the hands of Erma, it is likely that Dad is in deep denial over his own abuse. Therefore, having never come to grips with it during Erma's lifetime—and likely having never confronted her about it—it is now that much more difficult for Dad to heal emotionally.

17. "Mom fell through a rotted step and went tumbling down the hillside. She had bruises on her legs and arms for weeks. 'My husband doesn't beat me,' she'd say when anyone stared at them. 'He just won't fix the stairs.'" (Chapter 41, Page 185)

    With this quip, Mom tacitly acknowledges the extent to which neglect is its own form of abuse. Indeed, the most traumatic memories for Jeannette do not involve her sporadic whippings at the hands of Dad, but rather the starvation and deprivation the children suffer because of their parents' refusal or inability to provide for them. The situation with Mom is a bit more subtle, given that she, too, is both an active and a passive conspirator in the children's neglect. Perhaps this is why she approaches her accident on the step with a measure of gallows humor and a lack of seriousness.

18. "By 'us' I knew she meant the other black people. The pool was not segregated, anyone could swim at any time—technically, at least—but the fact was that all the black people swam in the morning, when the pool was free, and all the white people swam in the afternoon, when admission was fifty cents. No one had planned this arrangement, and no rules enforced it. That was just the way it was." (Chapter 43, Page 190)

This quote is a disturbingly effective expression of how de facto *segregation works in the American South. By this point, federal courts and legislation had prohibited lawful segregation, yet a decade later, segregation persisted in states like West Virginia because deeply ingrained racist attitudes and customs are difficult to break. Moreover, public facilities found ways to facilitate segregation while still maintaining a formal veil of colorblindness, for example by charging pool users a small fee during peak hours.*

19. "'Pillars shaped like women,' Lori said. 'The ones holding up those Greek temples with their heads. I was looking at a picture of some the other day, thinking, Those women have the second toughest job in the world." (Chapter 47, Page 208)

Around this point in the book, Jeannette finally begins to acknowledge how difficult it is for Mom to prevent Dad from siphoning off the entirety of the family's finances in service of his drinking and gambling habits. From this perspective, the fact that Mom can devote any money at all toward bills and food is a minor miracle. The quote also reflects the surplus of empathy Lori feels toward Mom, at least compared to Jeannette's attitude toward her, thus better contextualizing Lori's closer relationship with Mom in New York.

20. "For the first time, I had a clear idea of what Mom was up against. Being a strong woman was harder than I had thought." (Chapter 48, Page 214)

While Jeannette has already acknowledged the hardship Mom faces with respect to Dad, she does not truly understand it until she is charged with handling the family's finances while Mom and Lori are away for the summer. As a child who clearly needs affection and nurturing, Jeannette always favored Dad over Mom, who rarely offered much in the way of emotional validation. This realization is thus an important step in Jeannette's broader emotional arc, in which she lets go of her delusional admiration for Dad.

21. "Dad said he was damned if Feigenbaum didn't make a persuasive case that turbulence was not in fact random but followed a sequential spectrum of varying frequencies. If every action in the universe that we thought was random actually conformed to a rational pattern, Dad said, that implied the existence of a divine creator, and he was beginning to rethink his atheistic creed." (Chapter 59, Page 261)

So much of Dad's attitudes and behavior are seen through the lens of turbulence and order throughout the book. He is both an agent of chaos and one who basks in chaos. By framing turbulence as just another part of a broader orderly pattern too complex for mortals to perceive, the book reframes Dad's entire approach toward life. It is perhaps telling that following this epiphany, Dad's allegiance to chaos is briefly broken during his stint of sobriety and gainful employment upstate—a period that only ends when Mom convinces him to return to New York City.

22. "But Mom and Dad were clearly proud, and as I listened to them talk—interrupting each other in their excitement to correct points of fact and fill in gaps in the story—about their fellow squatters and the friends they'd made in the neighborhood and the common fight against the city's housing agency, it became clear they'd stumbled on an entire community of people like themselves, people who lived unruly lives battling authority and who liked it that way. After all those years of roaming, they'd finally found home." (Chapter 62, Page 267)

This is the closest Jeannette comes to defining her parents' philosophy. Their actions have always clearly reflected a strong antipathy toward authority, conformity, and boredom, yet much of their nomadic and self-destructive behavior often comes across like chaos for its own sake. By finally finding a community of likeminded individuals with a shared adversary to battle, Mom and Dad can finally root themselves to one place.

23. "I was thunderstruck. All those years in Welch with no food, no coal, no plumbing, and Mom had been sitting on land worth a million dollars? Had all those years, as well as Mom and Dad's time on the street—not to mention their current life in an abandoned tenement— been a caprice inflicted on us by Mom?" (Chapter 64, Page 273)

This revelation calls into question many of the possible reasons behind the Walls family's transience and indigence. It cannot all be the result of Dad's

*alcoholism, or Mom's artistic ambitions, or the pair's
shared hatred of conformity and authority. The truth is,
Mom could have at any moment ensured that Jeannette
and her siblings would never go hungry or suffer a cold
winter ever again, yet she chose not to. At no point does
Jeannette try to explain this decision, which may be
frustrating to the reader—yet the truth may be that
Jeannette's guess is no better than the reader's.*

24. "We hadn't gotten together since Maureen's
    arraignment. Something in all of us broke that day, and
    afterward, we no longer had the spirit for family
    gatherings." (Chapter 66, Page 277)

    *In the family's failure to gather in the wake of
    Maureen's sentence to a psychiatric facility, there is a
    tacit acknowledgement of the extent to which the family
    failed the youngest Walls sibling. Jeannette is
    particularly devastated by Maureen's fate, having
    promised to take care of her always upon first holding
    her as an infant. While for a long time Maureen sought
    help from outsiders and thus was not overly reliant on
    her siblings, as a consequence she never forged the
    same strong bonds that exist between Jeannette, Brian,
    and Lori.*

25. "He looked at the dishes. I knew what he thought every
    time he saw a spread like this one. He shook his head
    and said, 'You know, it's really not that hard to put
    food on the table if that's what you decide to do.'"
    (Chapter 68, Page 287)

    *Again, the discussion over how much of the Wallses'
    hardship is a result of discrete lifestyle choices made by
    Mom and Dad is an uncomfortable one. In focusing on
    their personal responsibility, there is a danger of*

ignoring other factors like trauma, mental health, and substance abuse that contributed to the family's circumstances. In any case, this quote from Brian reflects the extent to which the Walls children may always feel resentment toward their parents, even as the children continue to thrive.

ESSAY TOPICS

1. What does the Glass Castle symbolize for both Dad and Jeannette? How does it play into the slow erosion of Jeannette's illusions concerning her father?

2. To what extent are the family's struggles the result of Dad's alcoholism? Clearly it has grievous effects on the family, but do you the think the Wallses would thrive if Dad simply stopped drinking? Why or why not?

3. In what ways does Mom and Dad's marriage represent a codependent relationship? How does Mom enable Dad's alcoholism, both implicitly and explicitly?

4. How do the family's Christmas celebrations reflect the family dynamics in any given year? Cite at least three Christmas gatherings and what they reveal about the family, particularly with respect to the relationship between Jeannette and Dad?

5. What is the significance of the Joshua tree? How does it relate to Mom's attitudes on parenting?

6. To what extent is Mom responsible for the family's impoverished circumstances? Is poverty a lifestyle choice of hers, or do you see her largely as a victim of Dad's abuse, toxicity, and neglect?

7. The members of the Walls family approach their hardship using a variety of different strategies. How do these strategies reflect attributes inherent to their personalities?

8. Do you consider the Walls children's upbringing as abusive? In what ways do Mom and Dad's actions result in abuse, either directly or indirectly?

9. The relationship between turbulence and order is a common theme cited throughout the book. Why are Dad and Jeannette both so fixated on this dichotomy?

10. Why do you think Mom refused to sell the land in Texas, when doing so would have ensured that no one in the Walls family would go hungry again? Does Jeannette herself have an answer to this question?

Made in the USA
Monee, IL
28 June 2021